Betting-Shop Blues

The Diary of a Manager

Betting-Shop Blues

The Diary of a Manager

GUS HOWES

Illustrations by

Garry Lawlan

The Pentland Press
Edinburgh – Cambridge – Durham – USA

First published in 1994
by The Pentland Press Ltd
1 Hutton Close
South Church
Bishop Auckland
Durham

British Library
Cataloguing in Publication Data.
A catalogue record for this book
is available from the British Library.

ISBN 1-85821-267-7

Typeset by Carnegie Publishing Ltd, 18 Maynard St, Preston
Printed and bound in Great Britain by Bookcraft (Bath) Ltd

In Memory of my Mum
who laughed at my jokes

AUTHOR'S NOTES

Racing and the opening of betting shops on Sundays are nearly upon us, but where the extra staff are coming from is difficult to determine.

Hopefully this book will help, for one only has to tell the great British public how awful something is and they are clamouring for a bit of the action!

With the exception of Nigel, Mike and Graham, who are friends of the author and agreed to 'appear' in person, 'the firm' and all other characters are fictional.

ACKNOWLEDGEMENTS

With grateful thanks to Dave Thomas of Kickabout Publishing for his help and advice. Although we never met, he started as a business contact and ended up as a friend.

Thanks also to June Elks who typed the manuscript quickly and efficiently and my relatives and friends – especially Dave Hedger – for their help and encouragement.

'Geriatric Jim' was in today. He's only about 25 but seems to have the mental and physical faculties of an octogenarian.

Typically, he gives me his bet, I ring it up, photograph it, complete several other transactions and drink a cup of tea – and I'm still waiting for his money.

I like work; it fascinates me.
I can sit and look at it for hours.

But though I crave for work, I still
like to be fair. I do not ask for
more than my proper share.

Jerome K. Jerome
Three Men In a Boat

THE SERIOUS BIT

Some people will think that this is the only part of my book worth reading as it is faithful to the Trades Descriptions Act and contains no feeble attempts at jokes.

Based on my experiences, this book is an account of managing a betting shop but, as the majority of people do not visit such places more than once a year, let me first set the scene.

During my early years working in betting shops in the 1960s the weather was worse than it has been in recent years.

Every winter we lost lots of meetings and often all we had to bet on was one afternoon dog meeting.

Sometimes weeks would go by with hardly any horse-racing in this country and the bookmakers, mostly small firms, would just have to tick over until things improved.

If there was an Irish meeting we covered that, but the customers, more discriminating than they are today, were reluctant to bet on something that they knew little about.

Over the years many of the small firms sold out to small multiples who sold out, in their turn, to Ladbrokes, Hills and Corals.

These three firms now dominate, having about half of the betting shops in the country, and it is largely their influence that has changed the betting industry.

For them, betting is seen as big business, not a hit and miss affair dependent on the weather.

Dog meetings are rarely cancelled because of adverse weather so the one afternoon meeting of eight races increased to two meetings of ten races at each, and bookmakers, by paying dog tracks to hold meetings, gradually increased the coverage at every opportunity throughout the year.

The big bonanza came when bookmakers managed to get changes in the law to allow television in betting shops. At first this meant just the televising of regular racing programmes from BBC and ITV, but it did not take them long to jump on the satellite bandwagon and now shops are showing several live meetings every day.

That, coupled with a lot of extra meetings from the two all-weather tracks that had been constructed, increased turnover, and then November 1989 saw the start of three more profit-boosting ideas – twelve-race afternoon dog cards, satellite racing from Hong Kong on Wednesdays starting at 11.45 a.m., and dogs from Brough Park on Fridays with an 11.09 start.

So not only did staff lose their meal-breaks on Saturdays and bank holidays when racing already went on all day, now there were a further two days a week when they were deprived of a break and, to make matters worse, not all firms paid their staff proper compensation for the extra work involved.

Fortunately, Hong Kong was discontinued during the spring of 1990 and not reintroduced in the Autumn, not, I suspect, because of staff complaints but because it was not paying; but we still have Brough Park on Friday mornings, though it starts a bit later.

However, racing from Ireland and South Africa are now regularly covered.

Yet despite all these extra meetings bookmakers were clamouring to be allowed to open on Sundays and during the week to cover evening racing; and now Sunday opening is on the horizon whilst evening opening has been allowed between April and August.

To their credit, my firm, who did not want evening opening but had to be competitive, gained the usual respect by trying to meet their staff's best interests whilst responding to the demands of a changing industry.

This book is clearly not about them. It is not about anybody as such, although I fear that some betting-shop staff will see a similarity between the worst aspects of their firms and those of Wynn & Profitt.

PRINCIPAL CHARACTERS

The Author:	Gus Howes, manager of a betting-shop.
The Family:	The wife, Pat The kids, Peter and Helen The wife's mum
The Customers:	Albert, Fr. Murphy, Jeff, 'Geriatric Jim', 'Joe Loudmouth', 'Old Joe'
The Firm:	(In order of usefulness)
The Managers:	Colin, Dave — friends of Gus Clive, Glen — other managers
The Cashiers:	Margaret, *attached to Gus's shop* Tracey, Jill, June, Mark, Sheila, Paul, Sue — *Relief staff*

The Robots:	Neil, Gus's Section Manager *Troubleshooter-cum-relief-manager-cum-dogsbody for ten shops.*
	Personnel Manager (or P.M.) *in charge of staffing the fifty shops in the district. Poor man*
	District Manager (or D.M.) *a real bundle of fun!*

JANUARY 1993

Eternal diets – The diary saga – Early racing problems – Recruitment problems – Reflecting on an 84-hour week – Eat your heart out Encyclopaedia Britannica. Who needs you? I've got Sue! – Our worst fears are realised – New bonus scheme – A breakdown in communications – Stores, more stores . . . and still more stores – I'm ill – Why I'm sick of the Greenhouse effect.

Friday 1st January

Margaret, my regular cashier is on holiday this week and I've got June instead.

She told me that it was her New Year's resolution to lose a stone in weight.

What, again?

Since I've known her she's probably lost her body weight twice over. She eats salads for two months and gives me weekly progress reports of how much weight she's lost.

It's a bit like listening to the average punter recounting his successes at backing winners, which makes you wonder why all the bookies didn't go broke years ago!

Whereas the punter will boast of the pounds that he has won, June boasts of the pounds that she has lost!

But eventually she gets fed up with her diet, or just fed up, and has a bar of chocolate.

If it stopped there it would be OK but then she practically lives on chocolate for a fortnight and the progress reports end.

Eventually the much thumbed calorie-counting book re-emerges and the whole process begins all over again.

June's response to my criticism is that I can't talk as I haven't got any spare room in my 44″ waistband, but I can't expect her to appreciate that it's different for a man.

He needs more calories for a start and then even if he's doing his level best to shed a few pounds there's some devoted woman feeding him up.

The only time I ever managed to lose any real weight was in my bachelor days when I spent twelve weeks at a residential college where the food was adequate but limited.

I felt fit for the first time in years but when I went home my mum was shocked at how thin I was and said that she hoped the neighbours wouldn't think that she wasn't feeding me properly.

In due course I put on all of the weight again and further attempts to diet only met with limited success.

Once I managed to give up all biscuits and cakes and cut down on my sandwiches and then I would go home and my Mum would give me two more potatoes than usual.

"I've given you a bit extra," she would say. "As you're on a diet you must be hungry!"

Saturday 2nd January

Neil, my Section Manager, rang me to tell me that he would be bringing the racing diaries on Monday.

That's quite efficient by his standards – less than a week late.

Monday 4th January

Neil rang to say that he couldn't make it after all.

Tuesday 5th January

A customer asked, "Where's my diary?"

"I give up," I said. "Where *is* your diary?"

Wednesday 6th January

That's Christmas over and I've forgotten to take down the decorations at work – all five of them.

Thursday 7th January

I carefully took down the decorations, saving them for next Christmas. If I'm allowed to spend *another* £5, we will have a *real* display.

Friday 8th January

Today we saw the return of Brough Park on Friday mornings at the usual time of 11.29 a.m.

So we've got Brough Park on Fridays and no lunch-breaks and lots of meetings on Saturdays and no lunch-breaks and managers' meetings every two weeks or so and no lunch-breaks.

Some firms pay their staff proper compensation for all this extra work but all we get is £1.80 per day lunch allowance, in lieu of a break, and with luck we may get time to buy some food and eat it.

Saturday 9th January

I wonder why we have so much trouble getting and keeping staff. How about this for a recruitment advert?

"Trainee Managers required. Rapid promotion possible. Ability to go without food and drink for long periods an advantage."

Monday 11th January

The diaries arrived – all four dozen of them. Last year I got a hundred.

The District Manager is having another of his economy drives.

Tuesday 12th January

I chucked out the festive red and white envelopes in which we were meant to put the customers' racing diaries and used plain brown ones instead, partly because the meagre supply necessitated the hand-out being as discreet as possible and partly because I thought it inappropriate to wish customers a 'Happy Christmas' in the second week in January.

Wednesday 13th January

We've been so busy at work recently that I've been exhausted by the evening. All I've wanted to do was to have my evening meal and watch television.

Thus I haven't felt like reflecting on recent reports in the sporting press that the Government are looking into the possibility of extending betting shop opening hours as part of general proposals to deregulate shop trading hours.

Things have quietened down now and I have been pondering the implications.

If changes include Sunday opening the 84-hour week for shop managers could be just round the corner and will inevitably change people's lives.

Managers will have to employ their wives several days a week, not only to solve their staff problems, but also to give them the odd moment to talk together.

Then there would have to be a crèche built in the back of each shop for their children.

I would expect bookmakers to resist the added expense of employing nannies, so windows would be necessary, not only so parents could keep an eye on their offspring, but also to allow the children an occasional glimpse of their father.

This would hopefully avoid embarrassing questions when they all went on holiday together, like

"Mummy, who's that man?"

Thursday 14th January

At today's managers' meeting, the possibility of being allowed to open for evening racing was discussed at length.

Some managers said they wouldn't mind if we opened at noon instead of ten o'clock but this was rejected.

It seems that there will be two shifts instead, although where we are going to get the extra staff from remains a mystery.

Most managers thought that if there are two shifts they will end up working both of them.

Friday 15th January

Margaret had the day off and June was in again.

She had a salad and an apple for her lunch and then said that she was still hungry and went out to buy some bananas.

She came back with three Mars Bars – and ate them all.

My enquiry as to whether these were part of her calorie-controlled diet met with no response.

Saturday 16th January

Like most shops, we need extra help on Saturdays. The ideal arrangement was when I had Andy to help with the settling but he is now needed elsewhere so I get Sue, another cashier, instead.

This saves me getting up to help on the counter but it means that I've got two cashiers who talk and I can't hear the results.

So I turn up the speaker and they talk even louder and I still can't hear the results.

However, every cloud has a silver lining and I never fail to learn something from all the chatter.

Last week I found out which supermarket sells the cheapest coffee, which florist sells the best pot-plants and the relative merits of holidaying in a variety of foreign countries.

After today, I reckon that there is nothing I don't know about slimming and slimming clubs.

Monday 18th January

If we wanted any more racing diaries we had to phone the District Manager no later than today.

I asked for another four dozen and he said that I might get three. (Diaries, not dozen!)

Tuesday 19th January

In a surprise move, Home Secretary, Kenneth Clarke, announced that betting shops will be allowed to stay open up till 10 p.m. between April and August.

Working for a bookmaker can seriously damage your social life!

Wednesday 20th January

A memo arrived giving details of the new bonus scheme.

Now there are four opportunities a year to get no bonus, instead of two.

Thursday 21st January

Another managers' meeting.

I reckon that 90% of our managers think that 90% of the contents of such meetings are a waste of time.

That this opinion hasn't got back to upper-management casts doubts on *their* theory that these meetings are useful in the communication process!

Friday 22nd January

I heard that we won't be getting any more racing diaries after all. The few extra ones have been diverted to our prestige shops.

If we only get a further four dozen next year, it could be a bit embarrassing. I'll have to say,

"Sorry, but you had one last year!"

Saturday 23rd January

Sue was in again and the weekly ear-bashing continued unabated.

This morning I learned which baker sells the nicest cakes and which local towns to go to so I can play bingo every night!

Then this afternoon Sue gave us a crash-course in ear piercing. I reckon that all I need now is a bit of practical experience so I couldn't get home quickly enough to tell Pat I was giving her first refusal.

She said it was very considerate of me to think of her, but she would rather not.

That's the trouble with my wife. She never wants to try anything new.

Perhaps the D.M. wants his ears pierced – or his nose!

Monday 25th January

I met Colin, a fellow manager, for a drink tonight and we were soon moaning about work.

He said that he had once seen a programme on television about a new policy that some manufacturing firms implemented, where instead of having lots of components in stock, they only order what is needed for a given short period.

This can save a lot of money and we wondered why our firm hadn't latched onto it with regard to their stationery supplies.

This is something that has been brought up at managers' meetings on several occasions, but the answer is always the same – it's too complicated to process lots of different orders.

So we muddle through, swapping things among ourselves. For instance, I've only got a small board but I still get a dozen felt-tip pens every month, which I pass on to other shops as I'm still using those left over from when we were taken over, three years ago!

Tuesday 26th January

After last night's conversation with Colin I had a look at my stores this morning and concluded that I could offer reasonable competition to the local stationers.

For instance, we've got 328 envelopes and we only use five a week, enough punters' pens to stretch for 300 metres, if anyone was silly enough to lay them end to end, and enough Tipp-Ex to paint a baby elephant (although the RSPCA might have something to say).

Then there are the bulk supplies of cleaning materials.

The principle is that it is cheaper to buy in this way, but one always uses too much washing-up liquid pouring it from a five litre bottle and it takes a long time for two people to use four dozen bars of soap.

With a race every two and a half minutes or so, we don't get time to wash.

Wednesday 27th January

The man with the supplies arrived, with five gross of punters' pens, six dozen envelopes, a bottle of Tipp-Ex and various other items that we don't need and haven't got room for.

What we *do* need is a bigger shop to store the stores!

Thursday 28th January

I started a cold on Tuesday and by today I felt really rough.

In any normal job I would have rung the Personnel Manager and told him and he would have said,

> "I'm sorry to hear that, old chap. You better have the rest of the week off, and we'll see you on Monday, if you're OK."

However, when you work for a bookmaker, there's a fair chance that they will be several managers short, anyway; so when you phone the P.M. and say that you are ill and want to go home, first there is an eerie silence, and then, as far as you can tell, he has a nervous breakdown.

Being the kind, considerate guy that I am, I figured that the P.M. had coped with enough nervous breakdowns lately, so I decided to struggle on despite feeling awful.

In the circumstances, I thought it was reasonable that the firm should provide me with tissues, so I raided the cupboard where the Section Manager before last had stacked his bulk-buy of toilet rolls. Only another forty-three to go.

Friday 29th January

I told the customers that we had a special offer today – a free germ with every bet, but they didn't seem very worried. I expect they all had colds too (and were off sick!)

Saturday 30th January

Well, that's another month almost gone. In the good old days we could take it easy in January as it was the best month for cancellations, mainly due to snow and frost.

But then the Greenhouse Effect came along and spoiled everything.

FEBRUARY 1993

Progress? – Some shocking tales! – Short staffed – Getting away from it all – A Sporting offer – Rather c-c-cold – Bad news – I'm a romantic at heart – Women! – "Geriatric Jim" – More bad news – No relief! – My secret plan – "We'll be all right next week" – A local crime wave – The cleaner's lucky day – I get into debt.

Monday 1st February

We received a letter from upper-management informing us that next month our delivery of stationery will include anything that we specifically ask for.

So, not only will we be getting all the things that we *don't* want and haven't got room for, but also all the things that we *do* want and haven't got room for – because of all the things we don't want.

I suppose that's progress of sorts.

This state of affairs has been brought about by the District Manager's economy drives where stores have been cancelled and shops have been running out of basic items like rubber bands and red pens and managers have had to go out and buy them at twice the price we normally pay.

Tuesday 2nd February

One of our ancient fan-heaters finally broke down and I took it to the electrical shop round the corner.

The electrician said that he would look at it, but when I told him that I managed the betting shop he started ranting and raving about wicked gambling and hell-fire.

So I told him that I didn't want it *that* hot, just the normal three settings, but he didn't even smile.

He reminded me of our District Manager. He doesn't like my jokes either.

Wednesday 3rd February

As Electrician Number 1 refused to be tainted by bookmakers' cash, I had to see Electrician Number 2 who operates from his house. He charged me a tenner for telling me that the heater had had it.

Thursday 4th February

I sent Margaret round to Electrician Number 1 to get a new fan heater and various light fittings.

I wrote out a list, although I thought it expedient not to do so on a betting slip!

Friday 5th February

I met Electrician Number 1 in the Post Office and told him that I didn't agree with his theology but I admired his principles.

We then had quite a friendly chat about his religious beliefs, at least until he tried to convert me. He doesn't drink, smoke, bet or watch television. I told him that I did all four.

He exploded again. Apparently if there is anything worse than being a betting-shop manager it is having as many vices as me, so clearly if there is any punishment worse than hell, someone who is both a betting-shop manager and as vice-laden as me certainly qualifies for it.

Saturday 6th February

Five meetings in the afternoon and because of staff shortages I worked with only one cashier.

So I was bobbing up and down all the time taking bets and settling bets, and because I was taking bets I was missing results, and because I was missing results I couldn't settle the winners so quickly, and because I couldn't settle the winners so quickly I couldn't take the next lot of bets.

In the end, I began to wonder what the symptoms of a nervous breakdown are, because I thought I might be having one.

Monday 8th February

I had arranged to go out for a drink with Colin and we invited Jean, one of our ex-cashiers, and her husband, to join us.

Jean duly arrived, on her own, an hour late, which prompted two enquiries from us regarding the unreliability of her watch and the absence of her husband, or vice versa.

She said that her husband had decided to stay at home, as we would only be talking about work all evening. He's a fair judge.

Jean said that she was surprised that the firm had survived without her and we said that it was touch and go for a while, as we ended up getting three people to replace her, one of whom stayed two days, and another, a fortnight.

We exchanged the usual gossip about who had left, who was thinking of leaving, who had fallen out with whom, and why the District Manager is a twit!

Then we got on to Jean's new job. Apparently it's a nice little number. She actually gets a lunch-break *every* day, or time and a half if she works it, *and* she's had three rises in a year without having to ask.

"A bit like us," groaned Colin.

Tuesday 9th February

Glen, one of our whiz-kid managers and a member of the District Social Club Committee, phoned to invite me to an Inter-District football match one Sunday next month.

I declined an offer to be in the team and said that I didn't want to go as a supporter either.

My resolve weakened slightly when he told me there was a bar but I lost interest when I learned that this wouldn't be open until after the match.

To stand on a muddy, windswept field for an hour and a half in the middle of March, for the privilege of being able to buy a couple of pints afterwards is hardly my idea of fun.

The powers of persuasion apparently know no bounds and I was then offered the chance to be a linesman. This was a slightly better offer, for instead of standing on a muddy windswept field for an hour and a half in the middle of March, one avoids freezing to death by running up and down.

However, once again I refused the offer despite pleas to do my bit.

"We're desperate," said Glen, which sounded like the Personnel

Manager begging me to cut short my holiday and go into work because of the latest staff crisis.

Glen was only slightly easier to shake off than the P.M.

Wednesday 10th February

The firm insist that their managers wear a shirt and a tie, and if they wear a pullover, it has to be a V-neck one. But I've rebelled. It's so cold in our place that I have been wearing a round-necked pullover which didn't please the D.M. when he visited me this morning, soon after I opened.

"You know you're meant to wear a tie," he said.

"I am," I replied, pulling down the neck of my jumper and risking hypothermia.

I told him that it takes two to three hours to warm up and that I would conform with the rules when he conformed with the law which states that premises should be 16 degrees Centigrade after the first hour.

He said that he would see what could be done, which was what he said last year.

I don't really know why he came but I think I know why he left – it was to get back in his nice, warm car!

Thursday 11th February

The P.M. phoned me today to tell me that I couldn't have all of the holidays that I had requested as they had already been booked by other managers.

What a blow!

I make great efforts picking my holiday weeks.

Ideally the Saturdays all have five or six afternoon meetings, the Mondays are all bank holidays and there is evening racing every night.

Back to the drawing board – or rather, the racing diary.

Friday 12th February

It's a bit silly at our age, but I bought Pat a Valentine, otherwise she will only sulk.

It's a right rip-off though – 70p for a card that probably only costs a few pence to produce.

I wonder if the shop sells them off cheaply next week? Then I could buy twenty years' supply all at once, which would also save me the embarrassment of buying one every year.

I put the card on the front doormat before I went to bed. Pat will find it with the post in the morning. It's bad enough making the card manufacturers rich without lining the pockets of the Royal Mail as well.

Saturday 13th February

I only received one Valentine, an enormous card from Pat which cost more to post than I paid for the one I gave her.

She got six – five large ones (Peter and Helen are trying to wind me up as usual), and a small one (it's lucky one of us is economical).

Later the kids confessed to Pat that they sent *four* cards, getting their friends to write the envelopes.

Fortunately I can take a joke and there must be an innocent explanation for the other card.

Monday 15th February

I'll never understand women. Pat and I had a row about the extra Valentine.

Not because she got it but because I wasn't jealous and take her for granted.

When Peter got home from work he revealed that one of his mates had sent the extra card for a laugh.

I didn't think it was funny.

Tuesday 16th February

"Geriatric Jim" was in today. He's only about 25 but seems to have the mental and physical faculties of an octogenarian.

Typically, he gives me his bet, I ring it up, photograph it, complete several other transactions and drink a cup of tea – and I'm still waiting for his money.

"Oh," he mumbles. "I meant to ask for a price."

I write it on his receipt and photograph it and then have to hunt for the original, getting the rest of the bets out of order in the process.

Then I take a few more bets and at last Jim gives me his cash and then wanders off, in a trance, without his change.

Then he gets a winner and comes out of his dream world briefly, bringing up his ticket as soon as the result is announced.

"It's not ready yet," says Margaret.

"No hurry," says Jim, and stands at the counter drumming with his fingers and getting in everybody's way.

Then he wanders off for thirty seconds and with great ingenuity manages to lose his ticket and then stands at the counter looking through all his pockets and getting in everybody's way again.

Then someone finds it for him on the floor and we pay him out and wonder whether he will be having another bet or going home for his afternoon nap.

Wednesday 17th February

Managers' meeting. Given new contracts. We have to cover the night racing if relief staff aren't available.

We have a choice though. Sign it or get the sack!

Thursday 18th February

Six meetings in the afternoon really brings home the fact that working in a betting shop is very much of a waiting game.

We're waiting for races to go off and races to finish, we're waiting for the results of photos and stewards' enquiries, and we're waiting to help out on the counter during the next lemming-like rush.

Mostly, though, we're waiting with crossed legs for a suitable opportunity to go for a pee!

Friday 19th February

We've been sent details of the Inter-District football match, including a list of the fourteen players in our team.

I wonder if we can sneak them all on the pitch at the same time, without the other side noticing.

Saturday 20th February

The phone rang at 9.30 a.m. It was the Personnel Manager. He said that he had a staff crisis and we would have to work short-handed again.

"Sorry," he said, "a couple of cashiers have gone sick; it's only a one-off, we'll be all right next week."

I don't know how many times I've heard this prophecy but it rarely comes to pass.

Monday 22nd February

Jack had his bike stolen from outside the shop this evening and asked Margaret if she knew what time the buses went to town so he could report his loss at the police station.

Someone said he could have gone on his bike if it hadn't been stolen!

In the end Mac gave him a lift and it was from him that we learned that Jack described his bike to the police as "black, with a loose saddle, defective brakes and no lights!"

Tuesday 23rd February

Aren't our policemen wonderful. Jack got his bike back in less than 24 hours.

Apparently two officers in a patrol car had attended a minor accident last night involving a pedestrian and a cyclist who had been riding Jack's bike on the pavement.

The culprit thought that it was too dangerous to use on the road!

Jack should have been pleased but the police persuaded him to make it roadworthy and it cost him twenty quid.

This included a padlock, for, as Jack admitted, with all the new equipment it was now worth stealing!

Wednesday 24th February

One perk for the cleaner is that she gets first refusal on any lost property if it is not claimed within two months.

Normally she finds nothing but they say things come in threes and tonight she found 10p, a cabbage and a pair of false teeth.

I waived the two-month rule and said she could keep the 10p!

Thursday 25th February

I don't think the cleaner will be too disappointed to learn that the false teeth have been claimed.

Friday 26th February

I forgot to take any money to work with me, but we get £1.80 on Fridays in lieu of a meal-break, so I went round the bakers for my 'usual', which consists of soup of the day, a couple of rolls and a cake.

All the prices went up yesterday and I didn't have enough money.

Fortunately the lady decided to trust me for the extra 20p so I didn't grow weak in the afternoon, for lack of sustenance.

The only thing that doesn't go up is the lunch allowance!

Saturday 27th February

The P.M. rang to say that he was still short-staffed and couldn't give me another cashier.

"I'm taking on six new people," he said, "so we'll be all right next week."

MARCH 1993

My sad day – Old Joe the door rattler – An alternative Social Club – My birthday – The D.M. discovers that I'm less than perfect – Staff problems – The big match – Women and gambling – An unwelcome visitor – Our big pay rise – Some polite customers – A solution to the staff crisis (what staff crisis?) – A friendly visitor – Planning ahead for the Grand National – Jeff's attempt at the land-speed record – Albert's sad day – A young and bewildered cashier – A mid-week break! – A thoughtful customer! – Countdown.

Monday 1st March

With the promise of snow I was looking forward to a nice easy day but only Leicester was abandoned.

I like meetings being cancelled as I would rather be bored with too little to do than be bored with too much to do.

When Margaret came in, she said, "Anything off?"

"Only me," I replied. "I'm cheesed off!"

Tuesday 2nd March

9.55 a.m. I was putting up the papers when Old Joe tried the door. I looked at the clock – five minutes till opening time.

9.55,30 secs Old Joe rattled the door again. I looked at the clock and swore.

9.56 a.m. Another rattle. I gritted my teeth, counted to ten and then swore.

9.58 a.m. All his exertion had its effect and two minutes went by before he tried again.

9.59,50 secs I forestalled the next rattle by opening ten seconds early.

Wednesday 3rd March

The main item at today's managers' meeting concerned the forthcoming events of the District Social Club.

It was all so boring that I got to day-dreaming about starting an Anti-Social Club.

I got quite carried away – in my club there would be no football matches, no trips, no outings and no functions, but membership would be free.

We could have our AGM in a pub but I would have to insist that everybody bought their own drinks!

Thursday 4th March

My forty-third birthday.

I had indicated that anything of a gold colour that was also drinkable would be satisfactory presents and I wasn't disappointed.

Friday 5th March

There is a new PR exercise to test how polite we are to the customers and how efficient we are at selling the service.

Typically, an 'undercover agent' comes in, posing as a customer, we greet them and then they see if we can answer a simple question. For instance, it may be an enquiry as to whether a particular event is a tricast race.

If they ask the manager, or an experienced cashier like Margaret, all is well, but many cashiers' knowledge of horses doesn't extend much further than which end is which!

Anyway, the D.M. phoned this morning to tell me that the 'stranger' visited me yesterday and I only got 90% because I didn't say "good morning".

What does he expect from the President, Chairman, Secretary and Treasurer of the Anti-Social Club?

Saturday 6th March

The P.M. rang to say that we would have to manage on our own again.

Of the six new starters, three didn't turn up and by coincidence three other cashiers have gone sick.

But he said that we'll be all right next week.

Monday 8th March

Our first social event of the year, the Inter-District football match took place yesterday. I didn't go but heard all about it today.

As socials go, it was a disaster. The supporters' coach got lost and then it got stuck in a traffic jam and only arrived at the game in time for the last five minutes and, to make matters worse, another victim of the snarl-up was the man with the keys to the bar.

SPORT

By the time he arrived, the members of the Social Club weren't feeling very sociable.

In fact, the only sociable person around all day was our goalkeeper who let in fourteen goals.

Tuesday 9th March

A couple of young men came in last week with two young ladies. The lads were obviously showing off but the situation soon became strained.

"Why didn't you back that one instead?" said one of the girls, as "that one" romped home.

And the other one picked a good priced winner *before* the race, which her beau said had got no chance, and the poor fellow never heard the last of it.

The lads came in again today, but on their own. They had learned early in life that women and gambling don't mix.

The trouble with women is that they are always ready to tell you what you should back or what you should have done, but never ready to part with any money.

They will tell you to back something for them and you'll stand there like a lemon waiting for them to go to their purse, but they don't move a muscle.

So you think they will pay you later but the transaction seems to go completely out of their heads, unless they back a winner, of course, when they get all excited and stand over you demanding their winnings.

They've probably backed a 7/4 shot, each way, and you pay them out and they say, "Is that all?" and make you feel guilty.

But worst of all is the woman who's always moaning to her husband about all the money that he loses in the bookies, and what a fool he is, yet if she finds out that he's had a big win – *he would be a fool to tell her* – it becomes *their* money and she can't spend it quickly enough.

Wednesday 10th March

Some people are not very complimentary about District Managers, wondering what they do all day.

They say that when you want them you can never find them and when they are about as unwelcome as £1.79 on an unnamed favourite which dead-heats at 85/40 joint, Rule 4 applies they turn up.

Well, ours made an unwelcome appearance today and spent most of the time telling me things that I hadn't done properly

So I told him that I was like Frank Sinatra and liked to do things "My Way".

Notes:

"Unnamed favourite": some customers back the "favourite" which means the horse that ends up at the shortest price.

"Dead-heat": if your selection dead-heats, you lose half your stake and get the full odds to the other half.

"85/40": unusual odds, (two and one eighth to one).

"Joint": when customers back the favourite and there are two at a joint shortest price, the stake is divided equally between them.

"Rule 4": sometimes horses are withdrawn without

> coming 'under starter's orders', and money is refunded on these. It then follows that the chances of each of the other runners are improved, so their current or previous odds are inflated, so a deduction is made, on a sliding scale, based on the price of the withdrawn horse.

Thus, to explain the above diary entry, if one of the dead-heaters was one of the 85/40 joint favourites and the Rule 4 deduction was 10p in the pound, the customer would lose half of his stake because of the joint favourites and half of the half because of the dead heat.

So he would have a quarter of £1.79 at 85/40 (less 10p in the pound from his winnings).

44.75p wins 95.1p less 9.5p = 85.6p, giving a return of 1.30p including the stake (I think!)

If both of the dead-heaters were both of the joint favourites, the return would be £2.60.

Fortunately, such occurrences are rare!

Thursday 11th March

News of next month's annual wage rise has filtered through.

Apparently payments will be on a sliding scale.

I can guess what this means.

Friday 12th March

I was right.

Profits are up 6%.

Inflation is up 2%.

Our wages are up 1%.

Saturday 13th March

We were one short as usual and Margaret took about forty-five minutes to make a drink, in between interruptions.

Getting over the morning period is always the difficult part. There's one load of people wanting to get their horses on and another lot wanting to back dogs.

The net result is a fairly polite stampede in the direction of the counter.

In fact, some people are so polite that I find it difficult to take any bets . . .

"After you."

"No, after you."

"No, you were here before me."

Every time I grab for a slip it's withdrawn and someone else is invited to get on first.

My response to such genteel behaviour is to tell them to pretend that they're on the Underground in the rush-hour.

I expect they go away and tut-tut at my vulgarity before going home to luncheon of cucumber sandwiches.

For myself, I don't get time to eat in a civilised manner, so cucumber sandwiches are too indigestible!

Monday 15th March

Because of the personnel crisis the firm are asking existing staff to recommend satisfactory new starters from amongst their friends.

It might solve the staff problem but I wonder if our friends will still be our friends!

Tuesday 16th March

The general practice of Catholic priests making an annual visit to their parishioners went out some years ago.

However, the local parish priest is a traditionalist and still keeps up the practice, although he doesn't restrict his visits to one a year.

Indeed, he pops in to see my customers who are also his parishioners three days running every year and today was the first of those visits.

It was also the first day of the big three-day meeting at Cheltenham.

The Irish love their horses and their racing and take great pleasure in the Cheltenham Festival and Fr. Murphy is no exception.

Wednesday 17th March

With less than three weeks until the Grand National, the P.M. rang to discuss my plans for getting extra staff on that day.

Every year this proves a problem which is not totally unconnected with the firm's attempt to engage the best possible staff for the least possible cash outlay!

I will have to phone my mate, Alex.

Thursday 18th March

I rang Alex this evening. He's worked for me before on the big day but he only does it to do me a favour so I feel that we shouldn't take advantage of him as well, by paying him peanuts.

After a few pleasantries, I broached the subject.

"What are you doing on Grand National Day?"

"Oh no!"

"I'm desperate."

"You're always desperate. How much are you paying this year?"

"The latest offer is £25 clear. The firm pay the tax."

"Big deal. I get that at my ordinary job for half the hours."

"I'll get it up to thirty-five," I promised, knowing that the P.M. probably won't budge and I'll end up paying the extra tenner myself. Peace of kind can be expensive!

Friday 19th March

Since Jeff retired earlier in the year, he has his lunch in the Rose & Crown and then spends the rest of the afternoon in the betting shop.

The only complaint that he's got about the meals is that the service is a bit slow and he often misses the first couple of races.

Bet he likes a chin-wag and maybe that's what makes him late.

Anyway, he got to the shop today in good time for the third dog race just as a couple of his pals were moaning about the Council Tax.

So Jeff had to have his say – he didn't need many of the services that he was paying for as part of his Council Tax.

While he was holding forth, they announced that the hare was running so Jeff grabbed a betting slip, scribbled out his selection and rushed up to the counter.

Margaret and I have known him for years and it's not only money that goes back and forth but a variety of insults too.

"Late again Jeff," said Margaret, "too much chat and not enough action, as usual."

Then she told him that he was going senile and that he would soon need a few council services like a home help and meals-on-wheels.

"That's a good idea!" said Jeff. "If I had meals-on-wheels I could get them delivered here, then I wouldn't miss the first two races!"

Saturday 20th March

It doesn't make any difference that we're short-staffed and going like the clappers, there's still those customers with their special requests.

Someone asked to borrow the telephone directory and someone else wanted to know if we had any first-class stamps and then Albert arrived.

"Have you got yesterday's results," he asked, "and today's TV pages?"

He then stood in front of the counter waiting impatiently for me to drop everything and hunt around for them to save him spending 25p on a paper.

After a few minutes I managed to grab my copy of the *Racing Post* for him but he soon brought it back as it was yesterday's.

"Beggars can't be choosers," I mumbled to myself, adding in a loud voice, "hang on Albert, I'm a bit pushed at the moment."

During the next twenty minutes or so I was bobbing up and down taking bets and settling bets and each time that I went up to the counter there was Albert in the throng trying to attract my attention, whilst I was trying to pretend that I hadn't seen him. Eventually there was a lull but by then he had gone. I looked across the road and there he was coming out of the newsagents with a paper and no doubt a broken heart too!

Monday 22nd March

Margaret's on holiday this week and I've got Jill instead. She only started two months ago in one of our other branches but she was getting on pretty well and agreed to do a bit of relief work when we're stuck, which is quite often!

So she's been covering Margaret's day off and has already got to know a lot of my regulars.

I had to go to the Post Office and when I got back I saw Derek just leaving. He was laughing to himself and when he saw me he said what a right little joker Jill was.

I didn't have to ask Jill what it was all about as she looked puzzled and told me that Derek had been in and had said that he had won a monkey on Saturday.

Jill had thought it a strange thing to win and had asked Derek if he thought that it would get on OK with his cats.

I laughed.

"What have I said?" she asked.

So I explained to her that a monkey is racing slang for £500, but I promised not to tarnish her new-found reputation as a ready wit!

Tuesday 23rd March

Frank asked Jill to help him with his bet as his son who normally gets the job is away.

I knew what this meant and got up. Frank says that he "gets confused with this new money," so he writes out his bets in pounds, shillings and pence.

As we've been decimalised for twenty-two years, and as Jill is only 24, I figured that she might be a bit confused too!

Wednesday 24th March

Another managers' meeting. This time to discuss the Grand National on Saturday week.

I've done lots of them before but it's still a worrying prospect, although according to some anonymous person from upper-management, the whole emphasis should be on it being a 'fun-day'.

Presumably he hasn't got a shop to run.

At least he should follow the good example of our D.M. who deigns to come out of his ivory tower for the day to help out in one of the shops.

Thursday 25th March

Although we've been taking Ante-Post bets on the Grand National for weeks now, today saw the first of the once-a-year-brigade.

She said that she couldn't come in next week because she was on holiday and was it all right to put the bet on today.

I assured her that it was.

Then she wanted to know what to do as she had never been in a betting shop before.

I know her because she used to work in one of the local shops, but obviously she doesn't remember me because that's what she tells us every year!

Friday 26th March

Derek hobbled in today on crutches and with his leg in plaster.

He had fallen over one of his cats.

"Do you remember a horse called Hopping Around?" I said, but he wasn't amused.

If Jill had said that, I expect he would have thought it a huge joke and laughed so much till he fell over and smashed the other leg.

Saturday 27th March

Jill should have been with me today but the P.M. rang to say that he was sending me Mark instead, assuring me that he was an experienced cashier and used to working under pressure.

When Mark arrived he told me that he had only been with the firm a fortnight and had never worked one of my type of tills before.

So not only was I one cashier short, I had to teach the one I had got how to work the till before he could start.

This wasn't helped by Albert arriving and asking for yesterday's results and the TV pages.

He said that he had come before we got busy, as though he was doing me a favour!

Monday 29th March

Five days to go to the Grand National. Is there no escape?

Tuesday 30th March

We learned that the firm have condescended to pay us at time and a half on Saturday – for working twice as hard!

Wednesday 31st March

A poster arrived from Head Office with Saturday's opening hours: 9 a.m.–6 p.m.

I filed it in the bin.

APRIL 1993

An eggciting eggscapade – A difficult decision – Aaagh! Grand National Day – A helpful customer – Margaret's joke – How to get a day off work – "Joe Loudmouth" – Wow! I'm fully staffed – The delights of working over Easter – Celebrations all round – Evening opening – My misspent youth – A stupid punter – Silly me – I'm likened to the D.M. – How I nearly had a lunch-break – Neil fancies himself as a financial whiz-kid – Social club up-date – A thoughtful husband – I'm confused with the D.M. – A colourful day – How I failed in the incentive campaign.

Thursday 1st April

Boiled eggs for breakfast, or so we thought.

"This is a funny egg," I said.

"So's mine," said Peter.

"And mine," said Helen.

Then Pat broke into hysterical laughter in the kitchen. She had cooked scrambled eggs and put the empty shells in our eggcups.

How childish! (I wish I'd thought of it.)

A customer asked if we were going to open any earlier on Saturday.

"We open at nine," I said, "but don't tell anybody!"

Friday 2nd April

I deliberated long and hard as to whether to set my radio alarm for 7.15 or 7.30 tomorrow morning, deciding finally on the latter.

Saturday 3rd April

I woke up at four o'clock and spent the next three and a half hours lying there, worrying about all the jobs that I had left to do in the morning.

When I looked at my alarm for the umpteenth time it said 7.32 so I wondered why it hadn't gone off. I got up and investigated and found that I had set it for 7.30 at night.

The rest is history.

After working hard taking in the money, there were two false starts, the big race was declared void and we had to work hard paying it all out again!

At least Albert did me another favour by not asking for the TV pages *and* we were fully staffed for a change.

Monday 5th April

Somebody came in and said that he had had a bet on the Grand National but had lost his ticket.

I asked him to write out a copy of the bet but he couldn't remember what horse he had backed or how much he had on it.

The only thing he was sure about was that it was written with a blue pen!

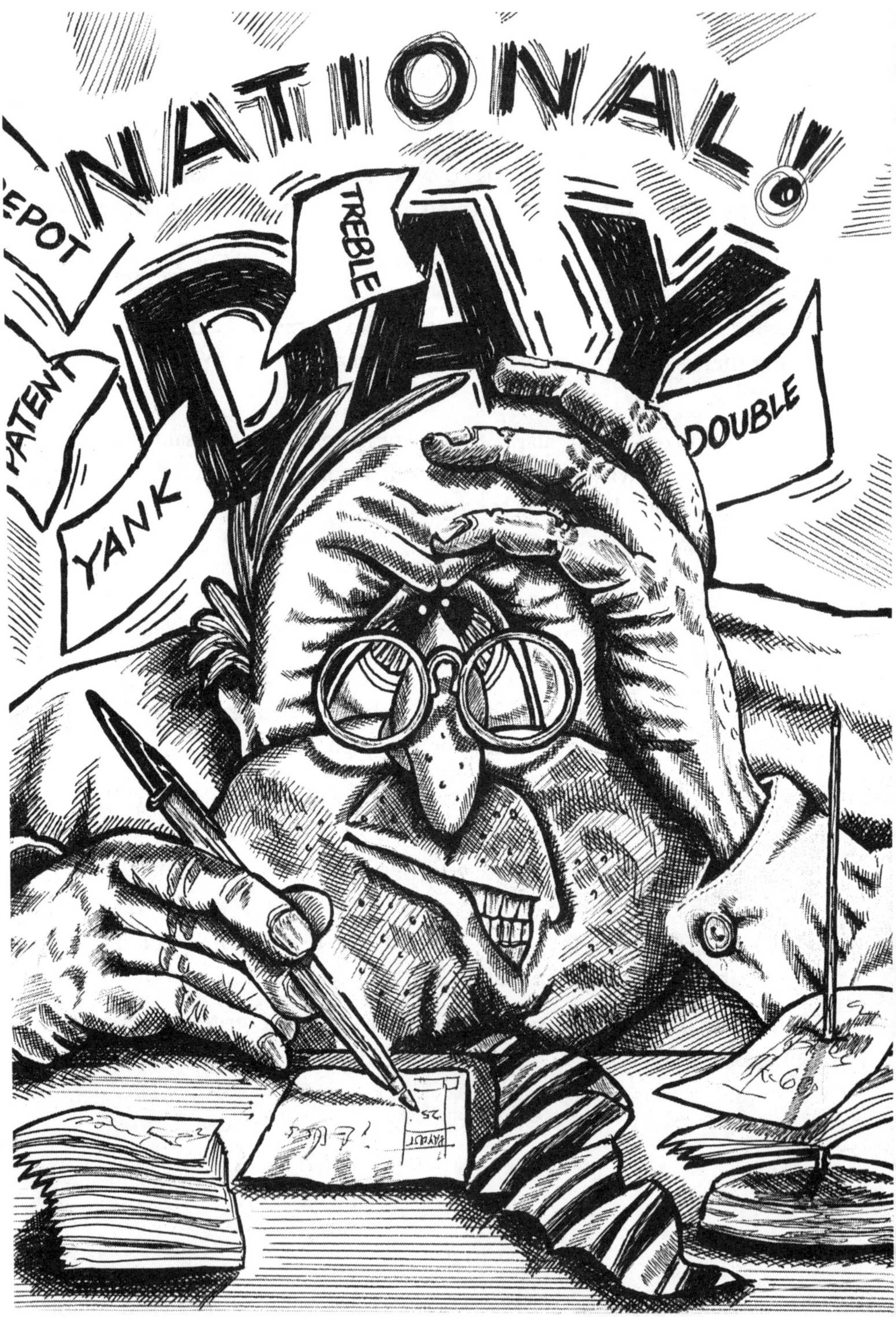

NATIONAL!
DAY
EPOT
TREBLE
PATENT
YANK
DOUBLE

Tuesday 6th April

A crowd of lads were in the shop today and were making a lot of noise. Clearly they had been in the pub.

It was just about tolerable until two of them started singing "Old MacDonald had a Farm," so I called out, "No animal noises in the shop, please."

Then Margaret added,

"Or you'll be baaaaaaaarred!"

Wednesday 7th April

The main item at today's managers' meeting was the *Racing Post* Betting Shop Manager of the Year. This is a very prestigious event and the firm are anxious to get as many nominations as possible.

It is an honour just to get a mention in the *Post* but anyone fortunate enough to get to the final gets a day at the Bookmakers' Exhibition in London in October, where the winner is chosen.

Dave said that he would be going all out to be a finalist this year as there seemed more chance of getting a day off work this way, than through the normal channels!

Thursday 8th April

I called at the Post Office before going to work because I needed some money for the weekend shopping.

As Thursday is pension day and as it was also the last day before the Easter break, the queue went past all the display units to the back of the shop and then doubled back on itself past the other side of the display units, where I joined it.

"Hiya Gus," somebody suddenly roared, and I knew it was "Joe Loudmouth"', one of my customers, but I couldn't see him.

"I'm over here," he shouted; and there he was, opposite me on the other side of the display units although about twenty ahead of me in the queue.

"It's a slow job," yelled Joe. "I've been here two hours already: I hope you've brought a book and packed lunch!"

He can be quite funny and does comedy turns at several of the local social clubs, being especially popular with those without microphones!

But there's a time and a place for everything and he never goes down too well in public because people are always worried that he will buttonhole them and talk, at the top of his voice, about all their private business.

The queue edged slowly forward but because we had started on opposite sides of the display units, the more the queue moved, the further Joe and I moved apart.

This didn't stop him from keeping up a conversation about his recent bad luck.

"Horses, dogs, football, you name it, I've always had bad luck," bellowed Joe. "It started on the day I got married."

He was back with his cabaret act, but I was rescued by one of his mates who came in to buy a paper.

"Hello Joe," he said, "had any luck lately?"

"Only *bad* luck," was the loud reply.

At last Joe got to the counter.

"Have you got a glass of water, love?" he yelled to the cashier. "There's a lady at the back of the queue who's fainted."

"Do you know," he continued, "I've been here so long, I've forgotten what I came in for."

But he was only joking.

When he had finished at the counter, the queue was longer than when I joined it. Joe told everyone to be patient as it *was* possible to be served because he had just proved it.

Then he suggested that we should have a sing-song to keep our spirits up, but I said that as there were still twenty people in front of me, I would rather save my strength.

Friday 9th April

Good Friday. No racing. Shop closed.

Saturday 10th April

Things are looking up. I'm fully staffed for the second Saturday running and the P.M. says that there shouldn't be any more cashier problems.

Managers are another matter. One has had to go into hospital and another is due to start jury service in a week.

The P.M. is hoping that in the circumstances the court will be sympathetic by putting off the latter's public duty for twelve months.

We'll probably have a similar problem then, but the P.M. is confident that "we'll be all right next year!"

Monday 12th April

Easter Monday

Someone called in this afternoon wanting to collect on a ticket from one of our shops in the next district.

"I didn't think we had one there," I said.

"It only opened a month ago."

So I checked the results in the paper, then rang their district office. No reply.

Then I looked through our list of local shops till I found one in their district and rang them for the number.

"Hold on," said the manager.

So I held on and heard him having an argument with one of the customers. It was getting quite interesting then the manager came back and gave me the number I wanted.

"Thanks," I said, "let me know how you get on."

"Eh?"

"With the guy who's going to write to Head Office."

"That's a joke – he can't even write out a bet!"

I left him to his problem and continued with mine by ringing the number he gave me.

"I've got one of your tickets from Saturday," I said.

"Hold on," replied the manageress, "I'll hand you to my cashier."

"Hello," said another lady.

"I've got one of your tickets for Saturday."

"Hold on, let me find a pen . . . OK, what's the number?"

I told her, then after a minute or two she came back to me.

"I can't find it," she said, "are you sure it's a winner?"

"Yes," I replied. "I've checked it with the paper."

She then went off again to have another hunt around, probably in the losers, then I heard her talking to the manageress and then a voice agreed the amount with me. All this took about ten minutes and although I managed to settle a few bets in between, I can do without that sort of thing on a Bank Holiday with 16 meetings.

Tuesday 13th April

One of the customers was talking to Margaret and me about all the racing over Easter and what a lot of extra work it meant for us.

"You've got it half right," I said, 'you should say, "what a lot of work it meant for me."'

Of course Margaret disagreed. She said that she had to take the extra bets, file the winners and pay them out; but I said that was all in her allotted hours, whereas I had to finish off settling the bets at home.

On both Saturday and Monday I did twelve hours although I only got paid for eight hours each day.

Yet, I suppose I should be thankful for small mercies. If the firm had their way we would have been open on Good Friday and Easter Sunday as well. (No doubt with the same arrangements regarding hours worked and hours paid for!)

Wednesday 14th April

Neil rang to tell us about our big quarterly bonuses.

Mine is £60 before deductions and Margaret's is £20.

We don't know what to spend it on yet.

Thursday 15th April

Colin rang to say that his bonus is £15 and he was going to have a party and blow it all in one big rave-up.

Friday 16th April

The first of nearly eighty nights of evening opening, although Taunton didn't really inspire.

Nor did having two lots of sandwiches!

I'll be getting a relief cashier in the evening but it looks as though I will have to do the night shift in addition to my normal day. Surprise, Surprise!

Saturday 17th April

The papers didn't come so I went round the newsagents to get them and was standing in the queue when I was reminded of my unchivalrous youth.

Amid the toys and novelties on display were string bags containing an unspecified number of marbles for 50p for, of course, the time between Easter and summer is traditionally the marble season.

In my younger days, you got 25 for 6d. although I didn't have to buy any as I was rather good at marbles.

I remember amazing my friends with some of my 'hits', halfway across the school playground.

One evening, one of the girls from my class came to see me and asked if I would sell her some marbles because she wanted to take some to school the next day. So I sold her 25 at the going rate and then challenged her to a game.

Half an hour later I had won them all back!

Monday 19th April

I served someone today who had added up his bet wrongly. It should have been two pounds more. I pointed this out to him and we agreed on the right amount and then I rang it up.

He then discovered that he didn't have enough money so we had to change the bet – and I had an over-ring.

What a bonehead!

However, I suppose we have to be patient. If the punters were intelligent they wouldn't try to beat the bookie in the first place.

Tuesday 20th April

The firm owed me a day off so I had it today and went into town to look around the shops.

I bought a few essentials like some cans of beer and some cigars and then decided to call in at our rivals and have a chat to the manager who used to work for us, until he got wise.

He wasn't there so I picked out some donkeys and had a 20p yankee, tax paid. When the cashier had rung it up I realised that I didn't have enough money left to pay the tax so she had to alter the stakes.

Silly me. But then anyone can make a mistake.

Wednesday 21st April

The District Manager attended this morning's managers' meeting in the function room of a pub.

We had just started when the juke-box from the bar blared out some pop music through the speakers in our room.

Neil got up to see what could be done about it and Dave, always quick on the draw with the jokes, called after him.

"See if they've got any golden oldies for Gus and the D.M!"

I thought it was quite funny but the D.M. was not amused.

Thursday 22nd April

I vary my lunch arrangements depending on what time Margaret starts and when the first race is. I don't go to the pub because I don't like drinking when I'm working but, as it happens, it's closed for renovation. As it was a reasonable day, I had intended on walking through the park, to a nice café that I know.

Then some guy came in at 12.45 p.m. and said that he had a bet with our firm in Birmingham yesterday and could he collect it from us.

He never had the shop number and he didn't know which area of Birmingham it was; all he knew was that it was near a double-glazing showroom.

As I'm not in the habit of going to Birmingham to check on the location of our shops, I rang our district office to get the phone number of one of them, which I rang.

"Is this one of yours? It's on the blue till etc. No? Do you know which of our shops in Birmingham is near a double-glazing showroom?"

They said it might be so-and-so and gave me the number, but it wasn't theirs but they gave me another number to ring and so it went on until eventually I got so confused that I was ringing shops that I had called before.

So I went back to the customer and told him that despite making about a dozen phone calls I couldn't find the shop.

He said not to worry about it as he was going to lunch and, anyway, although he had written the bet on one of our slips, he wasn't sure now if he had actually placed it with us, and perhaps he put it on in Northampton after all.

"Sorry," he said, and laughed.

I told him it was *quite* all right and that *I* was going to lunch until he arrived but it was too late now, and that it was early-closing day so the bakers would be shut, but if I got really hungry there were a few half-chewed dog biscuits in the car.

"But don't worry about it," I said.

He said he wouldn't, and left.

Friday 23rd April

Neil called in this morning and questioned me on my expenses with a view to cutting costs.

The only conclusion that he came to, after an hour, was that our use of one 14p rubbish bag every week was excessive and that we could save £4.68 per annum if we bought smaller ones which work out at 5p each, if bought by the gross.

Saturday 24th April

Margaret asked me if I had heard any more from the District Social

Club since the ill-fated football match; so I made enquiries on her behalf.

Apparently they nearly had a trip to the dogs, and they almost had a disco, and they would have had a coach outing if they had had the aforementioned disco to fund it.

But the good news is, that there may be a darts match next month if they can raise a team and find anyone to play against.

The net result is that April is nearly over and the Social Club have only had one more social than the Anti-Social Club!

Monday 26th April

Pat's birthday. I always give a lot of thought to her present so I thought and I thought and I thought but I still didn't know what to buy her.

In the end, I gave her the £20 voucher that the firm gave me for Christmas.

Tuesday 27th April

In *Three Men in a Boat,* the author accused George of "going to sleep at a bank from ten to four each day, except Saturdays when they wake him up and put him outside at two".

Such is life. No one can ever see below the surface of anyone else's job which is always described as "a doddle" or a "cushy number".

Today I was accused of working from ten till five with two hours for lunch.

I can only think that I've been confused with our District Manager who doesn't know what real work is all about.

Any fool can drive around all day, stopping off at our branches to annoy the managers and chat up the female cashiers.

I hear that when he gets back to his office he delegates everything to his secretary.

Now that's what I call a "cushy number".

Wednesday 28th April

The cleaner complained that the new rubbish bags are rubbish!

They are so flimsy that she had to use three of them instead of one of the others!

Thursday 29th April

One certainly gets excitement working in a betting shop.

Graham came in today with two tins of paint in a dodgy plastic bag.

The contrariness of life suggests that if he had tried to open them to do a bit of painting, he would have had trouble getting the lids off.

But as he wanted a quiet afternoon in the bookies, the bag split, the tins fell out and the lids came off, spilling paint all over the floor.

The effect was rather striking and in the right setting we could have charged admission to view the masterpiece, but my customers seemed unimpressed. But then I would expect them to be more at home with Stubbs than modern art.

Friday 30 April

I learned today that in our latest 0898 phone-line promotion, the winning manager registered 187 new clients, which was 187 more than me!

ALL MY OWN
WORK..
PLEASE GIVE
GENEROUSLY

MAY 1993

An elderly customer is disappointed – The prodigal son – Some good news! – How I got out of cutting the grass – I upset the D.M., Margaret, her dog and my wife – A welcome visitor – A welcome change – An unwelcome phone call – An enjoyable day – I welcome an expert's advice – Back to work – A not so enjoyable day – Why there is a long queue at the Post Office – Jeff's joke – An overgenerous punter? No! – Conflicting reports – Two happy managers – I'm shattered – Another bank holiday.

Saturday 1st May

I was talking to one of my elderly customers and he said that he called at the betting-shop the other afternoon but we were closed. Then he realised it was Sunday.

In the battle for Sunday racing the bookies may be able to enlist a new ally – "Help the Aged".

Monday 3rd May

Les called in today. He hadn't been in for years so I told him how grateful we were that he had condescended to pay us a visit.

He said that he now went to the rival establishment in town, as he didn't like our sixth of the odds a place when the favourite was odds-on.

I told him that we hadn't done that for ages; then Alf who had been quietly picking out his selections, suddenly piped up.

"He's like the prodigal son, just turning up when it suits him."

Les said that if he was the prodigal son, then he demanded his fatted calf, to which Alf replied that he thought he saw it tied up outside, unless that was Eric's Irish wolfhound, but why couldn't Les be reasonable and settle for a fifth of the odds instead.

I'll have to tell them that I tell the jokes around here!

Tuesday 4th May

The main item on the agenda at today's managers' meeting was the FA Cup Final next week and how we can promote it cheaply and effectively.

Neil gave us all some crêpe paper to see if we could make rosettes, then he went off to find the pub manager to pay for the room.

When he returned all our efforts had been in vain, so we decided to settle for decorating the shops in the team colours.

At the end of the meeting, Neil said that he had some good news and some bad news.

The "good news" is that we've got *another* managers' meeting next week, so I dread to think what the bad news is.

This will be revealed at the meeting on Thursday week.

Wednesday 5th May

Pat started nagging me at breakfast about the state of the lawn. She gave it its first cut this year and said that now it's my turn, but as my motto is "Don't do today, what can be put off till tomorrow,"

I said that I would do it later in the week, hoping that something would turn up to delay the inevitable for a few days.

However, I didn't bargain on what did happen.

I went to work, put up the papers, settled the bets, checked the cash and then put out the rubbish for the dustmen which the cleaner had left in three bags by the door.

They weren't particularly heavy but somehow I picked them up wrongly and hurt my back.

I'm a great believer in the principle that if you ignore something for long enough it will go away. This often works for some of the more tiresome exercises dreamed up by upper-management, but not, apparently, for bad backs.

As the day progressed, mine got worse and worse and I got more and more bent over until I could have put up a credible performance as the Hunchback of Notre Dame if it hadn't hurt so much.

I left the car at work and got a taxi home. When I got in Pat thought I was having her on as I didn't want to cut the grass. She only believed that I was genuine when I phoned my pals to say that I wouldn't be going on our weekly outing to the pub tonight.

Thursday 6th May

I was no better this morning so I rang the Personnel Manager and told him that I couldn't go in.

I thought it was very considerate of me to injure myself outside the peak holiday period, but he didn't sound very pleased.

Then I rang Margaret to get her to collect my keys and open up while the P.M. sorted out a manager and she didn't sound very pleased either. Nor did her dog, but then he never liked me.

He likes me even less now, as he didn't get his morning walkies.

Friday 7th May

The doctor has signed me off for two weeks and I was lying in bed when Pat decided to cut the lawn, although I thought that she could have been a bit quieter out of consideration for me, a poor invalid, or better still, she could have left it until I feel well again.

Not, of course, until I feel well enough to do it. I don't think I'll be capable of that again.

Later, I broke this gently to her, saying how sorry I was but I thought that in view of my bad back and the almost certain recurrent weakness, I thought that she would have to cut the grass in future.

"Huh," she said, "what's new?"

"Well, I sometimes do it."

"You did *half* of it once."

"We could have one of those nice brick patios instead," I said, to change the subject.

"It would cost a lot."

"Not if we did it ourselves."

"What about your bad back?"

"Well . . . er . . . when I said *we* . . . I . . . er . . . really . . . meant . . . er . . . *you*."

"Thanks," she said, "I don't know why I married you. Your mother said you were useless and I never believed her. All I got out of the deal was a seven-stone weakling."

I told her to get her facts straight, I was a *fourteen-stone* weakling. She laughed. She married me for my jokes.

Saturday 8th May

I never thought that it would be so boring lying bed all day.

Sunday 9th May

I haven't been so bored since yesterday.

Monday 10th May

I was so bored this afternoon that I wished I was back at work, but on reflection, I think I must have been delirious!

Tuesday 11th May

The doctor said that I should stay on my back for as much time as possible during the first week, so when Colin heard that I was confined to bed, he said that he would call in.

He came tonight at about nine o'clock which was the earliest he could make it, after leaving work and going home for a meal.

Colin said that the firm have suggested that we write to our MPs asking them to back bookmakers' requests to be allowed to open on Sundays.

He said that he *had* written to his MP, but only to complain that he was already working up to twelve hours a day, often without a proper break and that he needed his Sundays off.

Wednesday 12th May

Colin called in again tonight. He couldn't stay but asked if I would be up and around by the weekend.

I said that I was sure that I would be, so he said that he would try to get a couple of other managers to join him and they would call in on Saturday evening with a few cans.

Now, *that's* the sort of managers' meeting I like!

Thursday 13th May

I've reached the best time of my indisposition. I'm bad enough to be off work but well enough to get up and watch television.

This has nothing to do with it being Cup Final Day on Saturday!

Friday 14th May

The P.M. rang to ask me how I was. I think that he was hoping that I had made a miraculous recovery and would be begging to be allowed back to work, but he was disappointed.

Saturday 15th May

Colin and Dave called round in the evening.

"Wasn't the football great?" I said. "I wouldn't mind a job like yours where I could sit back in the afternoon and watch TV!"

"I had it on," said Dave, "but all I saw was the action replays for the goals."

"I didn't see much more," said Colin, "there *was* racing on as well."

Colin works in a rabbit-hutch that doubles as a betting-shop and as if to prove that the day wasn't only about the Cup Final, he said that he completed his Saturday morning jigsaw puzzle with the papers, just finding room on the pinboards for two morning dog meetings, six horse-race meetings and the night dogs, when one of his cashiers asked if they were covering the Irish meeting.

They were, of course, and he hadn't put it up.

I was interested to know what the 'bad news' was at the managers' meeting.

Colin told me that it had leaked out that this was that the D.M. would be there, so during the meeting several managers were winding up Neil asking him what was the 'bad news' that would be revealed at the meeting.

The D.M. obviously knew what was meant and Neil knew that he knew and got more and more flustered.

The D.M. left early and Neil said, "I know what you lot were up to. For that your punishment will be, no more managers' meetings for the next four weeks!"

Monday 17th May

I feel well enough to go back to work, but fortunately the doctor knows best and he signed me off for two weeks.

Tuesday 18th May

I visited a rubbish tip tonight. Not the local one for household waste, nor one of the children's bedrooms, but my shop wherein a variety of relief managers have been let loose for the last fortnight. My enforced rest is at an end and my visit was to collect the keys.

I only meant to stay a few minutes but ended up transferring two weeks' accumulation of junk from my desk to the bin.

This included bits of newspapers, memos, empty envelopes and a half-eaten cheese and pickle sandwich.

Wednesday 19th May

Back to work determined not to lift anything heavier than a cup of coffee.

So far 34 people have asked me if I was better, and 27 if I'd had a good holiday.

Thursday 20th May

I saw the FA Cup Replay on TV this evening, although it wasn't as enjoyable as the first match. Possibly because I was getting paid for watching Saturday's game!

Friday 21st May

I called at the Post Office this morning and Mary, the cashier, was arguing with some old dear who wanted her pension.

"You've had it already this week, you're not due any more till Tuesday," said Mary for the third time.

Working in the Post Office is a bit like my job – it would be all right if it wasn't for the customers!

Saturday 22nd May

Margaret got up to make a cup of coffee.

"I'll have two spoonfuls in mine!" shouted Jeff.

This is one of his favourite jokes as he likes to remind us that our rivals in town have got a coffee machine for the customers, and we haven't.

Monday 24th May

Reg gave me his bet for £2.20 and handed over £3 and I gave him his ticket and 80p change.

He picked up the ticket but left the money on the counter.

"Change," I called out to him, but he made no response.

"Reg, I've got your change here."

Still no response.

"Reg," I yelled, "I've got your change here – and a deaf aid."

He didn't move a muscle so I left the money on the side until he came to the counter again.

He came up a couple of minutes later.

"Gus," he said, "you forgot to give me my change."

Tuesday 25th May

All the managers I have spoken to report little interest in evening opening.

Wednesday 26th May

A press release from the firm announces that evening business has been very encouraging.

Thursday 27th May

A memo from the firm states that if evening business doesn't pick up soon, some shops will have to close!

Friday 28th May

I've heard that two managers from our district are leaving.

One of the defectors has got a job as a refuse collector which pays better money for less hours.

He says that he's going from one load of rubbish to another!

Saturday 29th May

Working twelve hours on Saturday is terrible. I'm absolutely shattered.

I miscalculated someone's bet, overpaying him £20, not realising until it was too late.

If asked for an explanation I'll write "mental and physical exhaustion".

Monday 31st May

Another Bank Holiday Monday, when everyone has a day off. Well, nearly everyone.

When our children were young they were always worrying me to take them to the seaside or the zoo on such days because their friends were going.

I had to explain to them that I was working, but it wasn't worth going anywhere because of the traffic jams, but we would go somewhere, by ourselves, when I got my lieu day.

When their friends came home they would say what a lovely time they'd had; even the traffic jams were fun as they had played car games.

Despite trying to get my day off to coincide with the school holidays, the P.M. would usually say how difficult it was because of staff shortages, so could I leave it for a bit.

So I would leave it for a bit and then on one dark and dismal day in February when all the horse racing on the next day had been cancelled, the P.M. would phone and say, "I seem to remember that we owe you a day off. How about tomorrow?"

Caught completely surprise, I would mutter,

"Oh – thanks."

Of course, the kids were at school and Pat had promised to take her Mum shopping in the car and it was snowing and I would spend a miserable day at home watching forty-year-old, black and white films on TV.

Then I would go back the next day only to find that the guy who should have relieved me had gone sick and they had put in a trainee who had trouble settling a fiver at 7/4 because the batteries in his calculator had run out.

And of course most of the customers hadn't noticed my absence the day before and blamed me for all the mistakes.

The situation has only been alleviated by our children getting old enough not to want to go out with a couple of fuddy-duddies in their early forties!

JUNE 1993

Disillusioned – Two ways of getting rid of Jeff – I make a mistake – The D.M. proves his worth – Margaret's milestone – Another managers' meeting and we come up with plenty of ideas – A serious young man – I survive my indiscretion – Why I'm not like your average actual betting-shop manager – An easy day! – Another social – No expense spared – Upper-management's brainstorm – Some cutting remarks – Going to work on a tranquilliser – What a day! – How to upset the Managing Director – How a customer got his money back – The brains behind our organisation – Three unhappy managers become elated ex-managers.

Tuesday 1st June

When I first started working for bookmakers I thought,

"Great – in the betting-shop all day and getting paid for it."

This month I 'celebrate' twenty-five years working for various firms, but the glamour has worn a bit thin!

Wednesday 2nd June

DERBY DAY

I was glad that I had Jill in, as an extra cashier.

During a brief lull, she went out to make some coffee and Jeff called out that he'd like two spoonfuls in his.

"What was that?" called Jill from the kitchen.

Margaret answered.

"Jeff wants two spoonfuls of arsenic in his cyanide!"

Thursday 3rd June

Alf presented a ticket which was over three weeks old.

"£4.50," said Margaret.

"I think it's a bit more than that," replied Alf, "did Gus do it?"

"Yes."

"He doesn't usually make mistakes, so maybe it's right."

"I try to be perfect," I said, "but it was a great disappointment to me when I found out that I was the same as everybody else and subject to human error."

I checked the bet with my results pages and found that I had missed a non-runner and that he had another £1.10 to come.

Margaret paid out with a cry of "Objection sustained!"

Friday 4th June

It was quieter than usual, because the old people's day centre had organized a coach trip and a lot of my customers had gone.

When Jeff came in I said,

"I didn't think you'd be in today. I thought you'd be on the geriatrics' day out."

He pretended to be upset and said that he didn't come in to be insulted, but he *might* forgive me if I made him a cup of coffee.

"I'll do better than that," I said, offering him twenty pence.

"I'll *buy* you a cup of coffee from that nice bookies in town!"

Saturday 5th June

A memo from the D.M. informed us that we have to record the total number of slips and stakes, taken each hour, for every day this week. He could have told us *last* Saturday.

I've never been able to figure out why we need District Managers, and the number of crazy, time-consuming exercises dreamed up by ours clearly indicates that this has also crossed *his* mind.

Monday 7th June

Margaret reaches a milestone in her life on Wednesday. It's her fiftieth birthday and she's got the day off to be with her family.

"It's a horrible thought," she said, "it makes me feel old."

I looked for a card to send her but I couldn't find a nice one with *50* on it, so I bought some gold-coloured numbers to stick on an ordinary card.

Then I thought better of it and stuck a *5* and an *0* on the envelope instead.

On the card I wrote,

"Your secret is safe with me – and the postman!"

Tuesday 8th June

The latest incentive campaign is called 'Teamwork' and it is all about how managers can co-operate with their cashiers, and vice versa, for the good of the business.

There are prizes for the best suggestions and at today's managers' meeting, Neil fixed up two sheets of paper and invited us to write down our ideas.

Then he went off to find the pub manager and pay for the room.

The first list read:
"How the manager can help his cashiers":

1. By serving the customers while they read magazines.
2. By letting them do their shopping in the firm's time.
3. By allowing them to watch *Neighbours* on TV.
4. By letting them use the firm's Tipp-Ex when they are doing the *Sun* crossword.

The second list read:
"How cashiers can help the manager":

1. By keeping him supplied with coffee.
2. By mopping his fevered brow.
3. By checking his *Sun* bingo numbers.
4. By letting him look at their local papers, especially the 'Situations Vacant'.

Wednesday 9th June

Mark replaced Margaret. He's a nice lad and a good worker but he has absolutely no sense of humour.

He didn't laugh at one of my jokes.

Thursday 10th June

Margaret thanked me for my card and gave me piece of her birthday cake which I had with my coffee this afternoon.

It wasn't poisoned!

Friday 11th June

Pat gets up when the radio alarm goes off but I'm not at my best in the morning and I was lying there listening to some symphony or concerto or whatever it was, and thinking that there can't be many betting shop managers who listen to Radio 3 every morning and wondering whether this made me a member of the intelligentsia.

I used to listen to Terry Wogan on Radio 2, although I didn't like the music much. It was Terry's aimless chatter in between the records that I enjoyed.

When he went over to television, I switched to Radio 4 to listen to 'Today'. I used to get up when 'Yesterday in Parliament' came on as I find politics so predictably boring.

Whatever one side says, the other side disagrees with and one can just imagine Mr Major announcing a really valuable piece of legislation, like all betting shops having to close for a week in the summer, with staff on full pay, to make up for all the unpaid overtime that they do; and a Labour MP getting up and telling the Speaker that the honourable (or is it the 'orrible?) gentleman hadn't gone far enough and that he should extend this to everyone, whether they did unpaid overtime or not.

Eventually, I got fed up with 'Today' as I find conversation in the morning tiresome, even if I don't have to answer, so I tuned in to Radio 3.

We don't buy a paper at home but now I realise that I could be an intellectual I think I should get one to reflect this.

Better still, if I cancelled the *Sun* at work, I could get the firm to buy it, so long as I put the racing page on the wall.

I will have to see if any of the posh papers have bingo.

Saturday 12th June

Naas was abandoned and we had an easy day, covering only 74 races instead of 82!

Monday 14th June

A memo, dated last Monday, arrived today from the District Social Club, advising members that the darts match postponed from last month (because someone forgot to book the room), has been rearranged for tonight at The Red Lion.

As to which of the numerous Red Lions in the district, it is not clear.

Tuesday 15th June

I heard that very few people turned up for the darts match.

It is a shame that all the efforts of the Social Club Committee get so little response, but I'm sure their talents won't always be wasted.

I see a bright future for them in upper-management!

Wednesday 16th June

It was Old Bill's 95th birthday today. He likes feeding the birds so I got him a bird-table whilst Margaret had a special cake made and iced.

We took these round his house last night and left them with his wife as Bill was out.

Then this morning we decorated the shop with balloons, in his honour.

When he arrived he thanked Margaret for the cake and said that it was nice of the firm to buy him such a lovely present.

"Gus bought you that," said Margaret "All the firm paid for was the balloons!"

Thursday 17th June

A memo from upper-management. They have *"revolutionised the system of sending us stationery"* (their words).

"About time." (Mine)

We will be getting forms which we fill in each month with our requirements.

What could be simpler? I wonder what will go wrong.

Friday 18th June

Margaret was off yesterday and she came in today with her hair cut short.

Of course, I didn't notice.

The first person that she served was Mike who had got a 50p yankee up.

"I'm glad to see you had it off yesterday," I said to him.

"I'm not the *only* one who had it off yesterday," he replied.

"I'm glad *somebody's* noticed," said Margaret.

Saturday 19th June

Eric was in.

"I like your hair," he said to Margaret.

"Crawler," I called out to him.

"Don't be jealous, Gus," he replied. "I like your hair too!"

Monday 21st June

The tension of working in a betting-shop gives me migraines but I've been successfully treated for these by my doctor during the last two years. I've got to take a tablet every day which means getting a repeat prescription from the chemist every couple of months but if it keeps the problem at bay, it's worthwhile.

However, the trouble has been recurring lately, but when you work in a betting-shop you can't very well down tools in the middle of the afternoon and go home.

So I told the P.M. this morning that I wasn't well and he said that he hadn't got any spare staff and could I "hang in there?"

He rang again in the evening.

"How are you?" he said, trying to sound concerned for my welfare, although I suspect that he was more worried about being short-staffed tomorrow.

"My head's spinning and I can't focus properly," I said, "but apart from that, I'm fine!"

Tuesday 22nd June

I saw my doctor this morning and he decided to change my medication, then I called in at the chemist's with the prescription on the way to work.

I was pleased to see that there weren't too many people in there, although I wasn't pleased that one of them was "Joe Loudmouth".

"Hiya Gus," he boomed, "are you ill?"

I was holding my prescription and thought that it was like asking someone standing by a river, with their clothes dripping wet, whether he had fallen in; but I didn't get time to answer because the chemist arrived to serve Joe.

When their transaction was completed they made their farewells.

"Goodbye, Sir," said the chemist.

"Cheerio, Mate," roared Joe, then he nodded in my direction.

"Don't serve that bloke, he takes all our money."

All the customers turned round to see what evil was lurking between the hot water bottles and the cotton wool and mothers glanced protectively over their children.

"He doesn't take *my* money," said the chemist.

"No," I said, "you take mine!"

Wednesday 23rd June

The new tablets that the doctor prescribed for me are a knockout!

He said that I was to take one at night because they might make me drowsy, which is something of an under-statement.

My radio alarm was set at eight o'clock and I vaguely remember it going off and hearing snatches of music and conversation, but after an hour the radio is programmed to switch itself off on the principle that no self-respecting person could still be lolling in bed.

The kids had gone to work and as luck would have it, my back-up alarm – the wife – was away for a few days, visiting her sister.

I don't know when I would have got up if it hadn't been for some guy outside with a pneumatic drill.

I'll have to put the buzzer on for the next few days as I can't rely on the Council digging up the road every morning!

Thursday 24th June

What a day!

First there was "Mr Sorry". He gave me a bet for £5.17 and a £10 note.

"Sorry," he said, "I haven't got the right money."

"That's all right," I replied, and got out £4.83 change.

Then he said,

"Sorry. I'll give you the 17p."

So I threw back all the change and got out a fiver and waited for the odd money.

"Sorry, I don't seem to have it after all."

Then there was Old Tom who tried to break his own world record for getting the most "5p wins" on a single betting slip. Every time I added it up I got a different answer.

Then there was a "Dave the Rave" who always hands in his ticket before the S.P., then Albert arrived with a ticket for last Saturday week.

"I found it in my pocket," he said. "I must have kept it for some reason".

I looked in the winners. It wasn't there.

"No," I said, and offered it back to him.

"Throw it away," he said.

So I chucked it in the direction of the bin. About three hours later Albert returned.

"You know that ticket? I know why I was keeping it now. I had written a phone number on the back."

So I rummaged about in the bin but couldn't find it. What I did find three times was the sticky lid of Margaret's yoghurt – or rather it found me!

"What's that on the floor?" said Margaret.

"Where?"

"In the corner."

It was Albert's ticket.

Next was "Mr Hard Luck" who never seems to back the winners he means to. He misses seeing them in the paper or he writes them out and changes his mind.

Yesterday the phone rang just as he was coming out and he missed two winners. The day before, his car ran out of petrol and he missed his 'banker' which won at a nice price.

He never seems to miss losers because of all these misfortunes. Today he actually got a yankee up but he still wasn't happy.

"I originally wrote out a super yankee with those four and another winner," he moaned.

Margaret's very good and always says something encouraging but I just get impatient with him and feel like saying that "sympathy's extra!"

It takes all sorts to make a world but why do they all have to come in my shop?

Friday 25th June

A big brown envelope arrived. Inside were four copies of the firm's 1992/3 Financial Report, on the cover of which is a picture of the Managing Director looking rather pleased with himself.

This was not surprising as he usually looks contented and he *was* announcing record profits.

I told Margaret that we could have two copies each, but she took one look and groaned.

So I hid a copy in one of her women's magazines so she would find it when she got home as I feel that she should take an interest in such things.

I put the others at the bottom of my in-tray.

Saturday 26th June

A memo arrived from head office.

"Due to holidays and sickness, any managers who wish to work a week of their holiday may do so by agreement with their Personnel Manager."

Perhaps the Managing Director would like to run a shop for a week. That would take the smile off his face.

Monday 28th June

We were very quiet this morning when a customer came in and handed me a ticket.

"I'm sorry, it's rather old," he said.

I suppose he thought that covered it being rather tatty too.

The date was 3rd April – Grand National Day – and I could just about make out the number which enabled me to locate the bet.

"£2.20, Sir," I said. "At least you've missed the queues!"

Tuesday 29th June

When races are off we put a special slip through each till to record this. These have the highly original name of 'off-slips'.

Someone once said that when upper-management were thinking of a suitable name for them, they took a week to decide on this, but I think that he was just being unkind and it may have only been a couple of days.

My shop is a small one with two tills and Ben's shop is a big one with two tills. Here the similarity ends. On Monday to Friday he has two cashiers to my one, as he takes twice as many bets as me.

As a result, he gets twice as much stationery as me. But he doesn't cover twice as many races as me so he doesn't need twice as many off-slips, but we can't expect *too* much from the people who decide these things!

I've never got enough off-slips and Ben's never got enough felt-tip pens, so at today's managers' meeting, ideas weren't the only things exchanged!

Wednesday 30th June

There are two major differences to being in Colditz and managing a betting-shop.

The first is that we've got a front door key and the second is that we're allowed home once a day.

Even so, the "escape committee" is alive and well and after news of the two recent successful bids for freedom, we've heard of another three escapees.

The D.M. has denied that we have reached crisis point despite the five defectors being around ten per cent of his managers, despite asking staff to work their holidays and despite bringing in relief staff from other districts.

It would appear that it is only a crisis when the D.M. cancels *his* holiday and runs a shop.

JULY 1993

Racing in the blood – My big bonus! – Two clever ideas – I upset a customer – Where there's muck there's money – I enjoyed going to work – How upper-management took three and a half years to nearly make a decision – A clerical error – At last! A fan! – The cleaner tries to be helpful – Jeff's dry wit! – No money for the minnows? – Two solutions to a difficult problem – I upset the D.M. – Pretensions of perfection – An infrequent gathering – How working in a betting-shop helps one to understand international problems – How I got the brush-off! – Wishful thinking – I start a new diet – "Joe Loudmouth" backs a winner – Ain't life wonderful.

Thursday 1st July

Alan was in this afternoon – the fourth time this week, which is pretty good going as it's only Thursday.

He used to work for us as a manager but when he got married he decided to get a different job, first because working for a bookmaker encouraged him to bet and, second, so he could have Saturdays off to spend more time with his wife.

So he got a job in one of the local factories, working nights, which gives him every afternoon off to do odd jobs around the house.

Well, that's the theory – in practice he spends most afternoons in my shop.

He doesn't come in on Saturdays though as he's got a part-time job – in a bookies!

Friday 2nd July

I calculated our bonus up to the end of June. After the hiccup in the first quarter it is back to the usual four figures – 0000!

Saturday 3rd July

During a brief lull in the proceedings this morning, I was standing at the counter when I noticed Harry going through his pockets. First he tried his side trouser pockets, then his back trouser pockets and then those in his jacket and after going through them all three times he got out his money and searched through that and then took out some papers and hunted through them and then looked around the counters and poked about in the bins.

At last he came up to me and before he could speak, I said,

"Don't tell me, let me guess – you've lost your ticket."

"How did you know that?" he exclaimed.

I told him that I was psychic and then said that he would have to fill in a form and I gave him the lost ticket pad which looks more complicated than it really is.

One look at that and he started another frantic search and then suddenly said,

"Ah, what's this? Here it is."

That form must have magical properties. We just have to show it to people and those lost tickets pop out as if from nowhere.

If you can believe what they say in their advertisment, partaking of a pint of a well-known brand of lager would prove just as effective and be more enjoyable, but at least our method is cheaper and can be used when the pubs are shut.

Monday 5th July

Some guy came in today with a ticket from one of our London branches.

He didn't know the area of London and he didn't have the shop number.

All he could tell me was that it was near a pizza restaurant and the manager had a moustache.

It wasn't clear whether it was the manager of the betting-shop or the manager of the restaurant who had the moustache, but in either case it wasn't very helpful.

The customer got annoyed when I said I couldn't pay him.

Tuesday 6th July

Dan was in today and he gave Margaret a really grubby fiver for his bet.

"What's this?" she said, laughing and picking it up gingerly by the corner. "I should refuse to take it."

Dan's next bet was for £2.20 and he gave her three one-pound coins.

"I hope these are acceptable," he said, "I've polished them all for you!"

Wednesday 7th July

I really enjoyed going to work this morning. The sun was shining, the birds were singing and there was a gentle breeze blowing through the car window. I was at peace with the world.

I got the same sensation going home too.

Pity about the bit in between!

Thursday 8th July

At today's managers' meeting Jack asked Neil whether he had heard anything more about relocating his shop to which Neil replied that the latest plan was to pull it down and rebuild it.

It probably wouldn't take much knocking down because it stands alone and is constructed mainly of wood.

In fact, it will probably fall down before upper-management finally make up their minds what to do.

When we were taken over three and a half years ago, they said they didn't like the shop spoiling their image and they were going to build new premises on the same site, but then they got worried about losing business during the rebuilding and decided to relocate instead, but they couldn't find anything suitable and again thought that they would rebuild, hoping that the customers would transfer to our other shop half a mile away.

However, the parking there is poor so they tried unsuccessfully for new premises and now they are back where they started.

Jack's shop features in nearly every meeting we have, not only the long-term plans but also the short-term mend-and-make-do operations involving Reg the handyman whose best efforts have stopped the premises from disintegrating, although he seems to be fighting a losing battle.

As soon as he replasters the walls or patches up the rotting floorboards, they need mending somewhere else. He's a good workman and although a stitch in time saves nine; you can't make a silk purse out of a sow's ear!

Jack said that Reg had just bought a new van and reckons that we have paid for it!

The main item at the meeting concerned betting opportunities on the British Open Golf that starts next week.

Neil is looking for an appropriate promotion that wouldn't cost a lot to set up and where it wouldn't seem amiss to give a prize of a lot less than the winner of the Open gets – say £20.

"I know," said Jack, "we could have a mini-golf tournament in my shop. The last time I examined the floorboards I counted eighteen holes!"

Friday 9th July

The stationery requisition forms haven't arrived yet so we won't be getting any stores this month.

I suggested to Neil that we wrote out our requirements on a piece of paper but he said that would be too complicated!

Saturday 10th July

Jill, my usual Saturday cashier went sick and the P.M. sent me Sue.

When she arrived she called out "You've got me today Gus, hard luck!"

"Don't worry, Sue," said Margaret, "he likes you coming – you're the only one who laughs at his jokes!"

Monday 12th July

I put up the display for the British Open Golf this morning and then this evening I asked the cleaner not to take it down as it had to stay up until the tournament was over.

"Right," she said. "If I remember I'll leave it up – but if it's gone one morning, you'll know I've forgotten!"

Tuesday 13th July

Margaret asked Jeff if he'd had a bet on the golf.

"I had one with the bookie in town," he said.

"Did you get better odds?" asked Margaret.

"No, just better coffee!"

Wednesday 14th July

The D.M. paid me a visit to discuss shop refurbishments and improvements. The good news is that he has £20,000 to spend. The bad news is that he has to divide this between fifty shops and the very bad news is that the high turnover shops get priority. When we discussed my requirements two years ago, I pointed out the dirty walls and asked if the shop could be decorated.

"Get a quote," said the D.M.

So I asked for a price from Ron the painter who is one of my customers. I sent this to the D.M. but I never got a reply.

Then last year I asked again about getting the shop painted.

"Get a quote," said the D.M, "and I'll let you know within a fortnight."

So I approached Ron again with the promise of an early reply – we're still waiting.

I'm still on speaking terms with Ron so today I asked for some new stools instead.

Thursday 15th July

At this morning's managers' meeting we discussed a recent memo which stated that certain posters *had to be displayed.*

What upper-management can't understand is that in order to respond to a poster, the customer first has to make his selections so if you're putting up posters instead of papers, you're defeating the object.

Someone said that in order to comply with the directive and so as not to lose valuable paper space, he had been forced to display posters in the customer toilet.

Colin said that perhaps this was taking the hard-sell approach a bit far and Dave reckoned that the customers would pee on the floor while reading the posters!

Friday 16th July

I've been reflecting on yesterday's managers' meeting and wondering how to comply with upper-management's directive about posters.

We haven't got a customer toilet and we've got a low ceiling so I can't put the posters above the papers.

My idea is that we should have mini-posters for small shops like mine. This would solve the problem and, in my case, hide some of the dirty walls!

If I suggest this, I've got two choices. I can either submit my idea through the normal channels; which means I tell my Section Manager who tells the District Manager, who tells the Area Manager, who lets the Directors know; or I can miss out the 'middlemen' and write to the Directors myself.

The trouble with the former is that it takes too long and is likely to get lost or thrown out on the way; and the trouble with the latter is that I'll get told off for not going through the normal channels!

Saturday 17th July

I was reading a letter from upper-management about being courteous to the customers when Jeff banged on the counter.

"You haven't got time to read – hurry up and take my bet or I'll complain to head office," he joked.

"Sorry, you miserable old git," I replied "I was just reading about being polite to the customers."

Jeff smiled but the D.M., who had arrived unnoticed, didn't appreciate my humour.

Monday 19th July

Pete was the only other customer when Bert came in and queried the amount we paid him on Saturday.

He had a super-yankee with three winners and showed me a bit of paper with the names of the horses and the prices.

I worked it out again for him and wrote the answer to each double and the treble on his paper so he could check it, then I told him how much I made it altogether and he said,

"That's what you paid me, you must be right then."

"I usually am," I said, smiling.

It was hot and the sun was beating down through the skylight to where I was sitting, so I made myself a sun-hat out of a page of *The Sporting Life*.

On seeing me attired thus, Pete said,

"They sell sun-hats in the shop up the road – but I suppose you couldn't get one big enough!"

Tuesday 20th July

My friends and colleagues, Dave and Colin, both live within a mile of me, but unlike me they don't work locally.

Tonight the three of us attended the first social of the Anti-Social Club in Colin's favourite pub on the edge of town.

None of us drink a lot but we would all have been over the limit so Dave got his wife to pick us up and run us there and then we shared a taxi home.

We may be anti-social but not anti-social enough to drink and drive!

Wednesday 21st July

Sometimes working in a betting-shop helps one to understand international problems.

Take the complicated situation that they have in Wales with all the Joneses. They solve this by having Jones the Post, Jones the Milk, Jones the Grocer, etc.

We have the same trouble with Georges. There's Big George, Little George, Motorbike George, Fitted Kitchens George, Scottish George and Big Jim's brother George, to name but a few of the thirty or more.

We heard today that George the Baker's wife has given birth to a baby George whom we look forward to welcoming as a customer

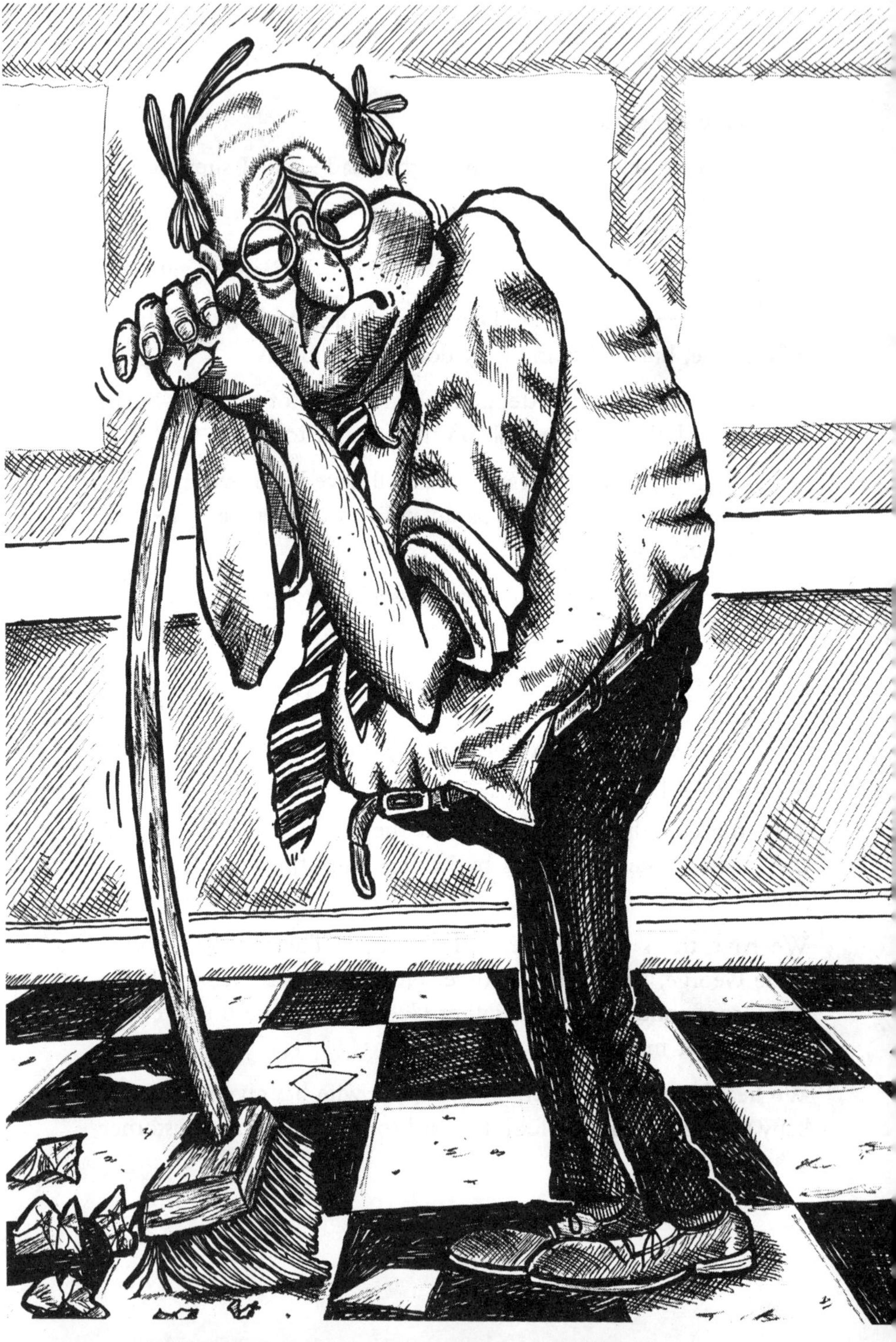

in eighteen years' time, though we will have to think of a new name for him by then.

Thursday 22nd July

The cleaner is away on holiday this week which is nice for her but rough luck on me as I've got to do her job.

I do most of it overnight but leave the sweeping up till the next morning and I was doing just that when Margaret arrived.

It was warm work and I was thinking that I wasn't cut out for manual labour, but even so I thought that I pushed the broom around with some style.

Then Margaret disillusioned me. She said that I reminded her of the story that she was reading her granddaughter the other evening.

It was about Mr Slow!

Friday 23rd July

"You're looking miserable, Gus!" said Bert.

"It's all this work," I replied, "I'll be happier in the winter when all the meetings are snowed off!"

Saturday 24th July

"I wish I could go home," I groaned as Margaret was replaced by the evening cashier at 5.30.

"Cheer up, Gus," said Margaret, "only another twenty-one years, seven months, nine days and one hour and you can retire – unless there's evening racing!"

Monday 26th July

A chip shop opened on the parade today, so I can get away from the repetitive diet of sandwiches.

I had cod and chips for lunch and pie and chips for tea.

Tuesday 27th July

Neil rang to tell me that the managers' meeting scheduled for this morning was cancelled.

"That's a shame," I said, "I find them really helpful."

Neil was quite taken aback by my enthusiasm but then he never did understand sarcasm!

Had sausages and chips for lunch.

Wednesday 28th July

It's getting very smoky in the shop so I've asked for the fans to be serviced.

Had saveloy and chips for tea.

If the smoke doesn't get us the cholesterol will!

Thursday 29th July

Joe Loudmouth gave Margaret his ticket for his Lucky 15.

"Just my luck," he moaned, "one winner and three seconds."

"45p." said Margaret loudly.

"Don't tell everybody," said Joe, "they'll all want a share."

"Well," replied Margaret, "you didn't put an 'x' on your bet for 'no publicity!'"

Friday 30th July

I felt remarkably cheerful today. Even the customers couldn't upset me.

Saturday 31st July

I was *even* more cheerful today. I'm on holiday next week.

AUGUST 1993

I tell a white lie – Gardening, shopping, decorating (some holiday!) – An improvement in the second week – The delights of going back to work – Rich pickings – Not one of my best jokes – Two customers are pleased to see me – I impress an innocent young lady – My money-saving idea – How one shop failed to open on time – The D.M. pays me a compliment! – The D.M.'s think-tank is a miserable failure – An old story – Eh?

Monday 2nd August

I'm on holiday for two weeks starting today.

I told the P.M. that I was going to tour Scotland for a fortnight which isn't true but I thought it sufficiently vague and far away not to be subjected to frantic phone calls to return because of staff shortages.

These can always be resolved by bringing in managers from other districts but it is expensive and plays havoc with budgets.

Tough!

Tuesday 3rd August

Cut the grass and the hedge, had a bit of lunch, then painted the living-room door.

I'm not used to all this manual labour. I'm exhausted.

Wednesday 4th August

With the paintwork in the living room looking nice, it showed up the drab-looking walls, so Pat decided on a shopping trip to buy some new wallpaper.

She also decided that I should accompany her, to help her choose.

I don't really know why she bothered to ask me. We spent about an hour looking at patterns and every time I made a suggestion she rejected it:

"That won't go with the carpet."

"I'm sick of that colour."

"You don't really like that, do you?"

"What about this one?" she asked. By then I was more exhausted than I had been yesterday.

"It's all right, I suppose," I said without enthusiasm.

That was enough and we bought it.

Thursday 5th August

Pat said that she didn't like the wallpaper that I chose yesterday so she's taken it back to the shop to change it.

Fortunately I was excused from going too.

Friday 6th August

If there's one thing that Pat and I are agreed upon, it is that she is better at wallpapering than me.

So I moved the furniture, then went to the pub and let her get on with it.

Saturday 7th August

Pat said that she would finish off the wallpapering this morning.

"I don't want you under my feet," she said. "Go out and buy yourself some new clothes – you're beginning to look like a tramp."

I obeyed orders and got myself a pair of trousers and a jacket.

When I got home I found a note from Pat. She had gone to her sister's and would be back later.

I tried on my new jacket and admired myself in the mirror. I don't think the wife will like it though – it doesn't match the wallpaper!

Monday 9th August – Friday 13th August

Pat and I belong to a rambling club but we prefer to go out on our own.

We usually walk four or five miles, stop at a pub for lunch and then walk back, but her leg has been hurting, so we cancelled the first and third parts of our daily excursions and drove to different pubs instead.

As for drinking and driving, we've got an arrangement: I do the drinking and she does the driving!

Saturday 14th August

The last day of my holiday so I called at the office at 6.30 p.m. to collect the keys from Dean, one of the latest intake of trainee managers.

The others are Wayne, Shane and Troy, so it looks as though Georges are an endangered species!

Monday 16th August

The main attraction of having two weeks' holiday together as opposed to two separate weeks is that you've only got to go back to one lot of mess.

On the other hand, after two weeks of freedom, it's that much harder to get back to the daily grind.

Margaret told the customers not to upset me as I had post-holiday depression *and* the Monday morning feeling.

This didn't stop Old Tom from querying his bet for "one day last week".

He said that he knew it was wrong when he collected it but thought it was better to leave it till I came back!

Locating slips paid out on previous days is never easy but one does hope for some assistance from the customer, but Tom couldn't tell me what day he had the bet, what day he collected it, the names of any of the horses or how much he had been paid.

The only thing he was sure about was that he should have been paid more.

The query was justified but what should have taken the perpetrator of the crime two minutes last week, took me half an hour this week.

Then it was down to clearing up some of the chaos left behind by the trainee manager who ran the shop for the second week.

The dates on the tills have to be changed manually. Not only has one got to remember to do this every evening before leaving but care has to be taken not to alter the month whilst changing the date.

This is clearly one area that our young whiz-kid has not yet mastered.

Successive days went, *Monday 9th August, Tuesday 9th August, Wednesday 9th August, Thursday 12th September, Friday 13th September, Saturday 13th August.*

The normal, boring calendar resumed today.

Tuesday 17th August

The stationery requisition forms have arrived, the managers have filled them in, the Section Managers have collated them and all it needs now is for the D.M. to authorise them.

Unfortunately he's off sick and it will be too late when he gets back.

I've only been back two days and I'm sick too.

Sick of work!

Wednesday 18th August

A memo from head office reminded us to promote football betting.

Although this only represents a small percentage of our turnover, it is always highly profitable because:

1. There is a relatively high margin in our favour for each game.
2. There is normally a stipulation that customers have to back a minimum number of selections.

   and

3. The results are unpredictable.

Thursday 19th August

Our marketing material for the new football season arrived.

The main selling point is how *easy* it is for the customers to win!

Friday 20th August

I went into town to do a few jobs, including calling at the opticians with my dodgy glasses and my brand new joke.

"I've got a screw loose!" I said.

The receptionist smiled weakly and said that she had heard that one before.

What a blow; I've been waiting weeks to use it.

Saturday 21st August

Bill and Tom only come in on Saturdays.

"Ah, Gus is back," said Bill.

"That other bloke was useless," Tom replied, "I had three bets last Saturday and he got them all wrong."

"Yes," said Bill, "he certainly made a lot of mistakes, but there was one consolation – he didn't moan as much as Gus!"

Monday 23rd August

I have the luxury of two cashiers this week.

Debbie has only been with the firm for a couple of weeks and as part of her training is working in Clive's shop and mine with the idea that the regular staff will have time to teach her the job.

She is young and pretty and I couldn't resist a few innocent flirtations, although I'm sure she didn't notice how hard I was trying to impress her with my wit and charm.

"Hello Debbie," said Pete, "what are you doing here? Aren't you in Clive's shop any more?"

"I'm working in both shops until I've learnt the job," she replied.

"It's much nicer here," said Pete, "not so much swearing."

"Not yet," said Margaret, "Gus is on his best behaviour!"

Tuesday 24th August

Our usual venue for managers' meetings have doubled their fee so Neil hired a room in the Community Centre.

The building is being extended outside and redecorated inside and there was a lot of noise from both sets of workmen which made it difficult to concentrate.

I suggested that we hold future meetings in the multi-storey car park near the motorway which would be both cheaper and quieter!

Wednesday 25th August

We had a losing day yesterday and I needed about three hundred pounds.

It's easier to get this from another branch than go to the bank in town, as parking is difficult.

So I phoned Clive at our nearest branch at 9.30, 9.45 and ten o'clock when we are meant to open. No reply.

Then I remembered that the District Social Club had, in their wisdom, arranged a disco for last night. This ended at 1.30 a.m. when the coach came to pick up the revellers and shuttle them back to their respective homes. With luck, Clive would have got to bed by about three o'clock. At least when you're President, Chairman, Secretary and Treasurer of the Anti-Social Club you get to work on time.

Thursday 26th August

Just my luck. While the D.M. was visiting me two customers queried their returns and I was wrong both times.

"Gus gets most of them right," said the D.M. to the second customer "because of the losers!"

Friday 27th August

Some weeks ago the D.M. suggested an idea to get some new managers.

This involves existing staff writing enticing advertisements, listing all the benefits of working for us, as opposed to rival firms.

Despite offering cash rewards for the most successful suggestions, nobody has so far had the imagination or the cheek to come up with anything.

Saturday 28th August

I met Colin and Dave for a drink tonight and we were discussing the D.M.'s ploy to get new staff and Dave said that he had sent in a suggestion which prompted the D.M.'s secretary to phone him and say that no one *except* him had contributed anything and no one *including* him had contributed anything worthwhile!

He wrote:

> *"Why work in a predictable, boring job where you get lunch-breaks and overtime pay and where the Personnel Manager is so predictably boring that you are always fully staffed?*

Enjoy the challenge of working for us instead.

Those who suffer from headaches, migraines, indigestion or nervous breakdowns need not apply."

Monday 30th August

Jill, who is firmly established as my second cashier on busy days, phoned the Personnel Manager a couple of weeks ago to ask if she could have this week off, bearing in mind that today is a bank holiday.

"That's OK," he said, "we've got plenty of staff."I thought it was too good to be true, then this morning he rang me to say that he had problems and could I manage with only one cashier.

"No," I said.

"Oh," he replied.

Then he went on to say that he could give me a second cashier but that would mean leaving another shop short which obviously put me in a difficult position.

Of course he told me that we will be all right on Saturday, but even if it's true it wasn't much help today.

Tuesday 31st August

If I had a fiver for every time I had to repeat something, I'd be able to take early retirement at 43.

Cyril came in with a bet and I checked the stakes.

"This isn't right," I said.

"Eh?"

"This isn't right, it should be £6.50."

"That's right," said Cyril.

"You've written £5.50."

"Eh?"

"You've written £5.50," I repeated loudly.

"I made a mistake," he replied, giving me £6.

"Another 50p," I said.

"Eh?"

"Why do I have to say everything twice?" I said.

"Eh?"

SEPTEMBER 1993

How I was two-timed! – It's a great life – How I was nearly nominated as Betting-Shop Manager of the Year – How I get a day off every week – A born loser – The idle poor – How I upset the P.M. and how he upset me – Broke – "Mr Skinflint" – An over-friendly cashier – The frustrations of ambition – A busy week-end – We get some new equipment – Not the sort of problem I have – I'm over-generous – A slight discrepancy – A language problem – Avoiding s-t-r-e-s-s – "Sodium Chloride".

Wednesday 1st September

Last night I noticed that the clock on one of the tills was two minutes fast.

This doesn't matter very much as we use "off-slips" to determine whether bets are in time but it is easier if the clock is right, so I unplugged it for two minutes.

Well, that was the plan, but it is easy to get distracted and I forgot to switch it on again, so this morning it was three and a half hours slow.

You can only advance it by flicking a switch and then, in a painfully slow process, it advances automatically a minute at a time.

When I went back to see how it was getting on, it had gone too far and was fifty minutes fast. So when I went to lunch I switched it off again. When I got back it was twelve minutes slow.

So I flicked the switch again and started counting the minutes as they clicked over, then someone asked me a question and I lost count.

When I checked the clock again it was two minutes fast!

Thursday 2nd September

Got up, went to work, had an argument with a customer, came home, watched telly, went to bed.

What an exciting life I lead.

Friday 3rd September

Nominations close soon for the *Racing Post* Betting-Shop Manager of the Year and to the best of my knowledge, nobody has voted for me, but then, I'm a modest sort of guy and haven't pushed my claim to being a superlative manager. One customer spoke of nominating me, so I offered to provide him with a stamp, an envelope, sufficient notepaper to list all my qualities and the loan of my fountain pen, but then I settled his bets wrongly two days running and he never mentioned it again.

Saturday 4th September

Someone who I hadn't seen before came in this afternoon and had a bet on a dog running this evening.

He gave me the impression that he knew very little about betting and betting-shops, which he confirmed by asking if we opened tomorrow.

So I told him that my employers wanted betting-shops open on

Sundays, the public wanted betting-shops open on Sundays and probably Mr Major wanted betting-shops open on Sundays, but as the law stood at present I was allowed that day off, to spend with my family and friends, and to rest my jaded brain.

Monday 6th September

Joe Loudmouth was in and got chatting to Margaret about sport. He said that the only one that he ever got actively involved with was boxing.

Joe stayed in the shop all afternoon and it was clear that his famous bad luck was playing its part.

The ones he backed to win finished second and the ones he backed each way were unplaced. If he did a straight forecast it came in the wrong way round and if he reversed it he got the first and third.

"With your bad luck you ought not bet at all," said Margaret. "If you don't get a winner soon we'll have to bar you to save you from further punishment!"

Tuesday 7th September

Night racing has ended for the year and at today's managers' meeting we discussed how popular evening opening had been.

In my shop we hardly had any really busy evenings and the mass exodus at 5.30 every night suggested that most people frequented betting-shops merely as somewhere to go until the pubs opened!

Wednesday 8th September

Sometimes the tension of working in a betting-shop gets to me and even my anti-migraine tablets don't work.

I've been bad since Monday but had managed to carry on, dosing myself up with paracetamol, but by this afternoon I realised that the only way to get well would be to have the rest of the week off so I phoned the P.M. and told him.

He wasn't exactly over the moon but made arrangements for me to hand over the keys tonight.

Thursday 9th September

I wasn't feeling much better today when the phone rang. It was the P.M.

"How are you?" he said, which is always an ominous opening gambit.

"A bit rough," I replied, trying to sound as ill as I felt.

"We're in a spot of bother," he said, "do you think you'll be able to work on Saturday?"

"I'll have to see how I feel tomorrow," I said.

If the doctor had given me two days to live I reckon the P.M. would have asked me to work one of them!

Friday 10th September

I felt a lot better and I saved the P.M. from another nervous breakdown by agreeing to work tomorrow. (I expect I'll have one instead.)

Saturday 11th September

Because of the security risk of keeping large amounts of money on the premises, we only keep enough to pay out any big winners and hope that what we take in covers what we have to pay out.

However, the bookie doesn't always win and it is not unusual to be cleaned out.

This happened today and we ended up with about fifty pounds in small change, having paid out all the notes and all the pound coins.

One elderly customer came in with a spring in his step, as he had won over a hundred pounds for a 10p yankee and staggered out leaden-footed with his pockets bulging with bags of change.

Monday 13th September

I phoned a couple of our shops on Saturday night enquiring about spare cash but they didn't reckon that they would have enough, so I decided to go to the bank in town this morning, before I opened.

I had settled the football and the dogs over the weekend as usual (as unpaid overtime), then I got to work half an hour early (more unpaid overtime), put up the papers, then left about 9.15 to get to the bank shortly after they opened.

Parking in town is always a problem and it took me about ten minutes to find somewhere, then I started thinking about what denominations of notes to get and what change, and then I thought that it would have been better if I had remembered to bring the cheque book with me!

I eventually arrived at work with the cash ten minutes after I should have opened.

The only customer waiting for me was Old Joe who was rattling on the door.

He often tries the door at 9.50 and then every minute or so until I open at ten. If I'm inside I find it infuriating but as I was outside I felt that I was getting my own back.

Margaret's on holiday this week, the relief cashier wasn't due in till eleven and I had indigestion, so I decided that I had better pop into the chemist's before I opened.

"It's no good rattling on the door," I called out to Joe, "he's not in yet!"

Tuesday 14th September

"Mr Skinflint" was in to pick up his winnings for last week.

I paid him £2.53 and he said that he made it another 2p.

He quite often queries his bets for a few pence and he's usually wrong but it wasn't worth doing it again so I gave it to him.

He really makes my blood boil. He doesn't need the money, it's just that he hates the thought of someone else having it.

Wednesday 15th September

I went out for a drink with Colin and Dave and who should I see in the pub but "Mr Skinflint". I thought that he would be too mean to drink.

He was at the bar complaining about getting short measures.

So he got his pint topped up and carried it over to his seat, slopping beer all over the carpet.

Thursday 16th September

The firm encourage us to be friendly to the customers but you can overdo it.

Dora and Doris are two of my regulars. They are both large ladies in their seventies, they always come in together and when they are not talking about horses, it's bingo.

As Margaret's away on holiday this week I've got Paul instead. He would be black-balled for the Anti-Social Club because he has got lots of chat and banter and really seems to take an interest in the customers, so although he has only been with me this week he knows that Dora and Doris like their bingo.

Part of his banter is bingo-based. If someone's got £11 to come, it's "legs eleven" and for £22 or 22p, it's "two little ducks, twenty-two".

But when two elderly, overweight ladies come in, one of whom has 88p to come, he should know better!

Friday 17th September

I heard that Terry, one of our managers who left a few months ago, has come back. The grass often seems greener on the other side.

It's like the seven daddy-long-legs that were on one of our windows at home this morning. Three were on the outside trying to get in, whilst the four that arrived yesterday must have voted unanimously that our house was pretty boring and were desperate to escape.

Saturday 18th September

I only had one cashier and got behind with the bets. I had instructed my slave to get my dinner by 6.30 and although slaves should be subservient, this one gets stroppy if I'm late, so when it got to 6.15 I knew that I would never get everything done in time so I stuffed the bets in my pockets and the accounting sheets in a carrier bag and left.

I got in, had my dinner and then started on my quota of unpaid overtime for the weekend.

I did the figures, then finished off the horses and then settled the football coupons, eventually finishing at nine o'clock.

I had started work at nine this morning and being something of a mathematician I soon calculated that that was twelve hours ago, and I still had the dogs to do, but I usually leave them till Sunday.

Sunday 19th September

With only one day off a week it is often difficult to find the time to fit everything in.

It makes you versatile though. Not many people can watch television, read the paper and eat their dinner, all at the same time.

Monday 20th September

We got two of the new computerised cash registers today, which records individual totals for horses, dogs and football (if we press the right buttons); gives the total bill for customers with a lot of slips (if we press the right buttons); records cash transfers and till-checks and blows raspberries at us when we do something wrong. (Although it's not *always* clever enough to tell us that we've pressed the wrong buttons.)

Tuesday 21st September

At today's managers' meeting we were told of a problem in one of Neil's shops.

It has been refurbished and now has some nice comfortable seats which have proved particularly popular with a number of local layabouts who have nothing better to do than sit about all week,

INCORRECT
LCD
HI-TEK
COMPUTERS
GUS

except when they *stand about* in the Post Office queue waiting to cash their Giro cheques.

Most of their sitting is done in The Rose & Crown where they are good customers, but when funds are low and the weather inclement they seek shelter in the betting-shop. Unfortunately, they occupy the best seats but don't spend any money.

In an attempt to remove them, the manager told them that he was sorry but they would have to leave because it is against the law to loiter on the premises.

They said that they were not loitering, but sleeping, or at least trying to, and suggested that he turned the commentary off as it was disturbing them.

Neil asked us if we had any solution to the problem, short of resorting to the law, and if any of us were experiencing similar difficulties.

"I've got a problem," said Dave, "fifty per cent of *my* early-morning customers never put a bet on and only come to sleep – two spaniels and a labrador!"

Wednesday 22nd September

The new computerised tills are increasing our turnover – if only on paper.

Today I got distracted in the middle of a transaction and rang up £95.95 instead of 95p, then £44 instead of £4.40 and finally a £200 bet instead of a £200 cash transfer.

Our takings didn't look too impressive after I took off over £300 of over-rings.

Thursday 23rd September

Terry gave Margaret several tickets, all of which were winners.

"£2.99 altogether," said Margaret, "have you got a penny?"

"Don't be mean," I called out. "Give him three quid. Be generous with the firm's money."

Friday 24th September

Not only were we cleaned out again, but when Margaret did her figures she announced that she was £492.02 short.

There's usually a rational explanation for such major discrepancies (most of it turned out to be an over-ring), so I made a joke of it.

"If we can't find it," I said, "I don't know how I'm going to break it to Neil. Perhaps the best approach will be to say,

> 'I've got some good news and some bad news – first the good news – we're skint!'"

Saturday 25th September

On Saturday nights I usually unwind by having a couple of beers at home and watching a video with Pat.

I decided on *The Sting*, but we had only seen about five minutes of it when she started.

"I hate American films because I can never understand what they're saying."

"I hate American films too," I said, "because I can never understand what they're saying because you keep saying that you can never understand what they're saying!"

Monday 27th September

I had the day off to go to the hospital to visit the neurologist about my migraines.

He told me what I knew already – that they were stress-related and that I should change my job.

I suggested to him that I should become his assistant and he could give me all the easy cases like mine which would give him time to concentrate on becoming a world-famous neurologist.

He said that he would have agreed if it wasn't for the health service cutbacks!

Tuesday 28th September

The P.M. phoned and asked me how I got on at the hospital.

I told him that I was to avoid stress which meant being fully staffed and not being given too much to do.

"Oh," he said, "I'll see what can be done – but not today. Margaret's off sick and I can't get a cashier over to you till 1.30 p.m."

Wednesday 29th September

The P.M. rang to ask me if it would be too stressful for me to manage on my own all day, as he was short of cashiers.

I've got a feeling that he doesn't really understand my problem.

I said it would be, so he said that he would get me someone before the first race.

I found out later that he took the sole cashier out of Glen's shop to send to me and made *him* work on his own.

Glen hasn't got a stress problem – not yet anyway!

Thursday 30th September

Margaret and I have worked in our shop for many years but we still don't know all the regulars by name.

To identify them among ourselves we give them nick-names.

There's "Michael Fish" who comes in every morning and wants to talk about the weather; "Tom and Jerry" who are always arguing, and "Robin Hood" whose usual moan is that he wins in the big, posh bookies in town and then loses it in our dump. (A classic case of robbing the rich and giving it to the poor!)

Then there's "Sodium Chloride" who earned his nickname because you have to take everything he says with a pinch of salt!

We see him for two or three weeks, then he disappears for about a month. He explains these absences by saying that he's in the Diplomatic Service.

He says that he can't talk about the work because it's all very hush-hush but he does reveal the various countries that he has been to and boasts that he speaks more foreign languages than the Pope.

Today we were visited by a foreign gentleman who asked us in halting English for a ticket, so I gave him a betting-slip.

"No, no, no," he cried and then broke into his own language which I thought was French as I had studied it, not very successfully at school.

Then "Sodium Chloride" walked in and I went over to him and asked him to help but he couldn't understand him either, suggesting that perhaps it was one of the Eastern European languages that he hadn't had time to master yet.

Fortunately, the chef from the new French restaurant came in for a bet and was pleased to hear his mother tongue and all was well.

His countrymen didn't want us at all. He wanted the travel agents but had been misdirected after asking for the "booking office".

Meanwhile, "Sodium Chloride" had disappeared. I reckon it will be for more than a month this time!

OCTOBER 1993

The D.M. proves he's not just a passenger – Foreign fiasco – Betting-Shop Limericks – Jeff's complaint – You can't teach an old dog new tricks – The firm try to be helpful – A quiet drink – What is worse than an offensive drunk – The perfect cashier – Changes in the culinary arrangements – Some clever clerics – A happy event – An eerie tale.

Friday 1st October

The D.M. paid me a visit this afternoon to ask if I had any problems and also to have a chat with me as to how I saw my future with the firm.

The only problem that sprang to mind was having to talk to him in between settling bets for five meetings, helping out on the counter, checking bets over the phone for a new manager and looking up what race meetings were on in the West Country next week for a customer who was going on holiday.

However, I didn't reveal my "thought-crime" to the D.M. who deigned to take three bets while I was on the phone.

As to my future, I said that I was satisfied with my shop and didn't want a bigger one, but if he ever felt that his job was too much for him, I reckoned that I could just about cope with it!

Saturday 2nd October

Not one of my favourite weekends. There was the Cambridgeshire today and the big French race, the Prix de L'Arc de Triomphe, tomorrow.

Taking bets on foreign racing is always something of a nightmare and we get involved in lots of tiresome conversations.

For instance:

Customer: *"What price is so-and-so?"*

Me: "10–1."

Customer: *"That's not very good. I'll have starting price."*

Me: "There's no S.P. on French racing. If you don't want our price, bets are settled at Pari-Mutuelle."

Customer: *"Pari-what?"*

Me: "French Tote."

Customer: *"Oh, all right then. I'll have Pari-whatsit. How many francs in a pound?"*

Me: (Sigh). "You don't have to bet in francs. The dividend is returned for one franc and we multiply that by your stake."

Customer: *(Sounding unsure) "Oh, I see – I want to pay the tax."*

Me: There's no tax on foreign racing."

(There is actually but we don't pass it on to the customers because the local taxes are taken before the dividends are declared which allows for the betting duty that bookmakers have to pay. However, I didn't want to have to explain all that – he probably wouldn't have understood it, anyway).

Monday 4th October – Saturday 9th October

I've been really busy this week.

Here is the result of my labours.

Betting-Shop Limericks
(Though it's no joke)

In the past there was likely to be
Time for the staff to have tea.
Then the boss cried, "A break?
There's been some mistake,
You're there to make money for me."

Those breaks were first whittled away
And so in real terms was the pay
At the time when the bosses
Complained of their losses
And said, "There'll be dogs every day."

Then the bookies soon cried, "We are through:
Why are the meetings so few?
Unless we win more
We are bound to stay poor
We'll increase the dog meetings to two."

They then saw more profits in reach
And decided, ten races at each.
Morning dogs were a ruse
To pay for a cruise
Or a trip to the sun at Palm Beach.

At this all the workers saw red,
"It's all a big con-trick," they said.
But our win soon proved hollow
When we had to swallow
Dog meetings at lunchtime instead.

Then bookmakers cried in dismay,
"There's no dogs on a bank holiday,
It's just what we need,
It's business, not greed,
Surely one meeting's OK."

There were Saturday dog bets to do
Plus horse and football bets too.
But then at half-ten
It started again
To ensure that the profits accrued.

It gave us a pain in the head
But there must have been bookies who said
"It really was wrong,
It went on too long,
We need two short meetings instead!"

The story continued to be
About how to make lots of money.
Teatime dogs soon ensured
That we wouldn't get bored
Although teatime for us, meant no tea.

Then, just as we wanted a snack,
Lunchtime dogs then made a comeback,
And it wasn't too long
Till we 'went' to Hong Kong
With no time to eat or to slack.

But the bookies still craved for more 'loot'
They said that the hours don't suit.
"Let's open at night,"
They cried in delight,
"For horses and more dogs, to boot."

"We should open each Sunday, also
We are sure the staff won't say 'no'.
Their wages are poor
And they'd like to earn more
But we'll sure work 'em hard for their dough!"

Monday 11th October

I've been experimenting with the newspaper display recently, altering the format to see what was best.

Today I got my first complaint, predictably from Jeff.

"It's getting as bad as a supermarket in here," he said, "you just get used to where everything is, then it all changes. The only change I *want* is a managerial one!"

Tuesday 12th October

You can't teach an old dog new tricks and I'm still not getting on very well with the computerised cash registers.

If we don't put the bets in straight, or do something else wrong, they blow raspberries and sulk till they get their own way.

I get my own back, though, by telling them lies.

When it comes up 'camera', which means, have I photographed the accounting sheets, I press 'yes'.

I'll do it – but only when *I'm* ready.

Wednesday 13th October

World Cup football: Holland *v.* England

The firm produced a coupon to make it easier and then changed the odds and told us to change all the coupons!

Thursday 14th October

I met Colin and Dave for a drink tonight.

We had thought of going to The Rose and Crown opposite my shop but I said that I would meet too many of my customers and I saw quite enough of them already!

I've only been in there a few times. On the last occasion I popped in I met Bob, one of my regulars.

"Hello Gus," he said, "I've never seen you in here before. I didn't know you were a drinking man."

"I don't like coming in," I replied. "I meet a lot of my customers and they only want to talk about horses and betting and I have enough of that at work."

"That's right," he replied, "you must get cheesed off with it . . . I had hard luck yesterday, I had three winners in a yankee and the last one let me down and then . . ."

Friday 15th October

Margaret had a day off so I had Jill today.

"What's worse than an offensive drunk?" I asked her.

She thought for a while and said,

"Two offensive drunks."

"Well – yes," I said, "but I was thinking of only one person, and he's just walked in."

It was Harold and he came up to the counter, swaying slightly.

"Gush," he said, "I've had a few drinks."

"So what's new?" I replied.

"Don't be like that Gush, I'm not drunk. In fact I'm as jober as a sudge."

Harold always comes up at the last moment, his bet is a load of scribble, you can't read the stake and he's never got his money ready. Apart from that he's a model customer.

When you find out what he wants, he is very apologetic but it is the same story every time. He's still late, you can't read his bet, he hasn't got his money ready and he apologises again.

When he eventually left, Jill breathed a sigh of relief and said,

BET HERE

"He's a nice man but tiresome, but surely not worse than an offensive drunk?"

"You can bar an offensive drunk," I said, "but you have to put up with a polite one!"

Saturday 16th October

Jill, our relief cashier, who usually works for me on Saturdays and in other branches during the week, was originally employed to work two days a week, including Saturdays, but because of staff shortages she has been doing five or six days every week.

She did not particularly want to work the extra days but the P.M. always gave her a tale of woe and said that this was his worst week and that he would be all right next week, but by then *that* was his worst week, and so it went on.

When Jill applied for her holidays she found out that she was only entitled to eight days for the full year because of her two-day contract. She hadn't earned any extra days' holiday by working more than her contract hours.

She was a bit annoyed although she accepted it, then asked the P.M. for a five-day contract instead, only to be told that she wasn't needed on a regular basis! He even refused to give her a three-day contract. So I wasn't surprised when she told me today that she had gone after another job and that maybe someone would ring me up for a reference.

I don't blame her but I'm not looking forward to working with only one cashier on a Saturday again, especially with winter coming on, when the morning dogs overlap the afternoon horses.

Monday 18th October

The dreaded phone call from Jill's potential employer came this morning and the guy sounded as if he had made up his mind and only needed a good reference.

I told him that Jill had the two essential qualities for working in my shop – she's an accurate cashier and she laughs at my jokes!

Tuesday 19th October

I got home from work to find that Pat had tripped over the kerb and hurt her knee and could hardly stand, let alone walk out to the kitchen and prepare the dinner, so the kids had cooked it.

It wasn't that good but I complimented them on their efforts just in case they told me that I could cook it in future.

"Thanks," said Helen, "It's your turn tomorrow."

Wednesday 20th October

Pat's knee had swollen badly so I rang the doctor and asked for a house visit, then I rang my mother-in-law who agreed to come round and let the doctor in as I had to go to work.

She phoned me later to say that they were at the hospital and that Pat had fractured her knee-cap.

I got home to find her with her leg in plaster.

Helen wasn't joking about me cooking the dinner tonight. Both her and Peter had gone out straight from work so we had incinerated sausages and scrambled, fried eggs.

Thursday 21st October

I called at the chemist's on the way to work and bought some Rennies.

I wasn't cut out to be a cook.

When I got home Pat said that the plaster had set and she could walk with the aid of a stick, so she could get the dinner ready.

"You relax, I'll do it," I said without thinking. "Is egg and sausage OK?"

However, the kids said that they would cook the dinner and I could wash up.

"Mum's got enough problems without getting food poisoning as well," said Peter.

To which Pat replied that one was more likely to get food poisoning when things were *under-cooked!"*

Friday 22nd October

Pat has taken over the catering again, much to the relief of the rest of the family.

She says it was nice being waited on but she got bored sitting around all day, doing nothing.

I know the feeling. That's why I like to get out on my day off (Sunday).

However, I don't mind sitting around doing nothing when I'm at work.

Saturday 23rd October

Jill has got the job and is leaving next Saturday.

She was chatting away with Margaret this morning so I turned up the speaker so I could hear the results, then Margaret complained that it was too loud.

I said that *it was too loud* but it wasn't the broadcast that was at fault!

Monday 25th October

Fr. Murphy came in with some fellow priests – friends of his from Ireland.

I don't know whether they had inside information, heavenly guidance or tomorrow's paper, but they were remarkably successful.

Tuesday 26th October

Fr. Murphy and his pals were in again before adjourning to The Rose and Crown.

I've heard that several lapsed Catholics have changed both their betting-shop and their pub!

Wednesday 27th October

The priests came in again to pick up yesterday's winnings. The visitors are going back today.

The takings will be down, but the profits will be up!

Thursday 28th October

Eric was in today with the photos of his latest grandchild.

For the fortnight before the birth Margaret was seeking daily progress reports, and when Eric finally announced that the happy event had taken place, she wanted to know all the usual details that women want to know about babies.

Apart from hearing that mother and child were both well I wasn't very interested, although I do remember that it's a girl, born last Saturday at 8.14 p.m. weighing 6 lbs 2 ozs and they have called her Dawn.

Considering the time of arrival, Eve would have been more appropriate!

Friday 29th October

When I got back from lunch, Margaret was talking to Jeff about the Halloween Party that she was going to tomorrow.

"I expect you're going as a witch," said Jeff.

"Just for that, I'll put a spell on all your bets," replied Margaret, "so you won't get any winners."

He didn't either!

Saturday 30th October

It was Jill's last day with us today, at least it was until the P.M. rang.

He was full of apologies, knowing what a busy day it was, but because of staff problems he needed her elsewhere and we would have to manage on our own.

It is at times like this that one appreciates the joy of missing the results because of two noisy cashiers!

NOVEMBER 1993

We score an own goal – I show some improvement – The D.M. gets hot under the collar! – A much delayed holiday – Our first walk – What was nearly our last walk – Three jokers – Back to work – I'm in receipt of a tip. (A rubbish tip!) – A perfect lady – I sense a coup – A fishy story – My long weekend – How upper-management stamp out waste – Two more fishy stories! – The highlight of the year – We give money away – How my ears burned – Upper-management. What would we do without them? – A dog's life.

Monday 1st November

I went in early to put up a display for the football promotion which takes place over the next four weeks.

The staff in the shop which does best get a meal out with the D.M., although there is a cash alternative.

No prizes for guessing what I will choose.

Tuesday 2nd November

My parcel of football coupons looked a bit thin. When I opened them I discovered a note which said that as we only took about 35 a week they were cutting our supply from 100 to 50.

Haven't these guys heard of wastage?

I tried to find Neil. It only took five phone calls which must be a record. I told him what had happened.

"It's a great bit of timing," I said, "cutting down my coupons the week we start a promotion."

Neil must be practising for a job as a District Manager. He wasn't any help!

Wednesday 3rd November

Tony the teacher queried his returns. He had a 2p forecast double up, but I had only settled it for 1p.

"Sorry Tony," I said, "but I got it half right."

"Never mind," replied Tony, "though I'm afraid you still get nought out of ten."

Thursday 4th November

When Tony the teacher came in, I said to him,

"I got your bet right yesterday, Sir. May I have ten out of ten *and* a gold star, please Sir?"

"No star, it was easy."

It was easy. It was a loser.

Friday 5th November

The District Social Club had a firework party tonight and burnt the D.M. in effigy, whilst the Anti-Social Club kept a low profile and had its AGM in our favourite pub.

We voted unanimously to restrict our official anti-socials to the nights when the other lot have socials and also to restrict our membership to three to avoid having a too sociable Anti-Social Club.

Dave proposed, and Colin seconded, a motion that our members should not, at any one time, hold more than two positions on the Executive Committee.

This was carried by two votes to one!

Colin is now secretary and Dave is treasurer.

I hope that this extra responsibility will not be too much for them.

Saturday 6th November

A few days before my planned holiday in February, the P.M. rang me and asked if I was going away.

I made the mistake of saying that I had nothing planned so he asked me if I could help out by working instead, as a couple of managers had gone sick.

So I'm off next week instead of that week and the following week which I had booked already, so I thought it expedient to go away somewhere this time just in case there is another staff crisis!

Monday 8th November

I've been having a bit of trouble with the car lately and I didn't want to risk taking it, so I went by train to Worcester to meet my friends, prior to travelling by road to Somerset for our walking holiday. I've always been a bit nervous about trains since I went from London to Oxford via Reading and London, but this time I managed to change trains without mishap!

The plan was to all meet at Nigel's house, then set off at four o'clock.

At five past four Mike, the other member of the party, rang to say that he would be there in ten minutes. So Nigel and I sat on the doorstep to wait for him.

That was a mistake. We should have stayed in and had a game of Monopoly instead!

Mike eventually arrived with a suitcase, a rucksack and a bag of books.

"Sorry I'm a bit late," he said, "I remembered at the last moment that I had to go to the library as my books were due back."

"You didn't have to get five more out," replied Nigel.

When I said "Let's go to Somerset and walk in the Mendips," my friends agreed, and Mike suggested that we rented a cottage.

Nigel and I reluctantly agreed as we prefer bed and breakfast in a guest house but we let Mike go ahead with his cottage idea on condition that he made the arrangements.

At least we can blame him if anything goes wrong.

Tuesday 9th November

We got up late, then after breakfast drove to Wells.

Then, attired in pullovers, quilted anoraks, gloves and woolly hats, we set off to enjoy ourselves.

Our initial objective was Wookey Hole which is only a couple of miles away but that didn't stop us from getting lost.

When we eventually got there we discovered that the caves were close to the pub, but it gets dark early this time of the year and we didn't have time to go in both.

As the caves are famous we will try to visit them another time.

We went back the way we should have come.

Wednesday 10th November

We visited Glastonbury this morning and walked up the Tor, at the top of which is the remains of a church.

It's quite a climb and I bet the locals were pleased when it fell down and they built another one in town.

After lunch we drove to Uphill where the church is also uphill, so we gave that a miss and walked the first three miles of the Mendip Way to Bleadon after first establishing that there was a pub there.

Thursday 11th November

This morning we drove to Cheddar and walked through the Gorge and then picked up the Mendip Way again which took us to the top of the cliffs.

On descending, we drove to Draycott for lunch and then walked to Priddy and back.

Altogether, we had about ten miles of walking which is about right.

Gone are our grandiose plans of yesteryear, like our first (and last) backpacking holiday.

On that occasion we went to Cheltenham where we had booked bed and breakfast.

In the morning, we assembled outside the guest house with our packs and, shrugging off taunts of "Everest's that way," we started our trek out of town.

Our first set-back came when we got lost in a housing estate; then I got tired and suggested that we pitch our tents in a playing field that we had just passed but my friends were made of sterner stuff and pooh-poohed my idea.

It was hard to imagine a better site, though. (I had been reading up about camping). The ground was level, there were no stones, nettles, thistles, trees or cows and there was (hopefully) a plentiful supply of water from nearby houses.

However, we pressed on and eventually got into the country and did another three or four miles before collapsing by the roadside.

To cut a long story short, we ended up at a bed and breakfast place, camping in their back garden.

After two nights of tent and breakfast, I moved into the house. Oh, the joy of a sprung mattress.

Nigel accused me of being a "part-time camper," but by that time I didn't care.

Nowadays, we are less ambitious. All we hope for is a nice walk and to get to the pub in time for lunch.

Friday 12th November

On hearing of our exploits, Graham, another friend, expressed an interest, but he couldn't join us until tonight.

I rang him this morning.

"What do I need to bring?" he asked.

"All you really need is a sleeping bag," I replied, "but Mike says to bring your guitar, and Nigel says to bring some money as it's your round!"

Saturday 13th November

We stopped off in Wells before today's walk as Mike wanted to buy a paper.

We had an enjoyable morning, getting to the pub in good time for lunch. Graham asked Mike if he could borrow his paper – a tabloid – which Mike handed over though he was rather surprised because Graham usually reads one of the posh papers.

He didn't read it though, but rested his boots on it "to save getting the carpet muddy".

Sunday 14th November

On the way to the starting place of our last walk, we stopped at some shops and I accompanied Mike who bought some apples, a paper and a box of groceries for when he got home.

When we got back to the car, he opened the boot, moved the rucksacks to make room for the groceries and then put the apples and paper in his bag; then he thought better of it and transferred the apples to Nigel's rucksack.

Nigel never noticed until we stopped for lunch.

Monday 15th November

We travelled back to Worcester today where I had planned to stay overnight at Nigel's house and then go home tomorrow.

When we got there, I phoned Pat to tell her that I had got back safely and she said that the Personnel Manager had rung and said that if she heard from me today, would she ask me to ring him at home as soon as possible.

I don't suppose he wants to know if I had a good holiday or tell me that I've got a rise, but having previous experience of frantic phone calls from the P.M. my guess is that there is another staff crisis and could I please postpone the rest of my holiday till next year?

I told Pat that she hadn't heard from me but I would ring him when I got home.

Tuesday 16th November

I got ten out of ten for predicting the staff crisis and nought out of ten for not completing my holiday and being a right idiot and agreeing to go back to work tomorrow.

Wednesday 17th November

Neil's been in my shop while I've been away and he is as messy as the rest of them. I separated the drawing pins from the rubber-bands in the rubber-band box and then did the same in the drawing pin box, and then put the pens and paper clips, which were scattered all over the table, where they belonged.

Then a customer came in with a ticket for Monday but I couldn't find it in the winners.

"Are you sure there's something back?" I said.

"I had a forecast double," he replied.

So I went over to the pile of papers that I keep for the results. In just over a week my nice neat pile of essential pages has become an untidy jumble of all the bits that haven't been displayed on the pinboards.

The paper on top was last Saturday's and then came last Wednesday's and then I found a bit of yesterday's but not the bit that I wanted.

I found the right bit by grovelling in the rubbish bag.

Neil rang me later from another shop to ask if I had Monday's results. He said that the bonehead who was there yesterday had chucked them out!

Thursday 18th November

It was Margaret's day off so the P.M. sent me Tracey who does everything by the book.

Her till sheets were a work of art and included the day, the month, the year, several copies of her signature and the full names, and their status, of all the staff who worked in the shop today (that is, both of us).

Before she went home she gave me the sheets to sign and I hardly dared touch them for fear of spoiling them with a grubby finger-print, nor did I like to sign them with my usual scribble, so I invented a handsome new signature that will confuse the security department.

I congratulated Tracey on the presentation of her till-sheets but told her that it wasn't necessary to include her religion; but apparently 'R.C.' stands for 'relief-cashier'.

Friday 19th November

"Why didn't you become the Betting-Shop Manager of the Year?" asked Jeff.

"The short answer is you didn't nominate me," I replied.

"I'll vote for you next year," he said. "We're bound to get rid of you if you win, because your firm won't let their Number One Manager stay in this grotty little shop."

"I like this grotty little shop," I replied, "it's just *certain* grotty little customers that annoy me."

Saturday 20th November

On winter Saturdays both I and the two cashiers order something from the fish and chip shop which John the manager brings along to us at about midday.

Although his menu is extensive, by coincidence we all ordered plaice and chips.

"Here you are," said John, on delivering our lunch, "a plaice treble!"

Monday 22nd November

On Saturday morning a customer asked what time we closed that night.

"Five o'clock," I said.

"Part-timers," shouted Jeff.

I let it go. I didn't tell him that I did at least eight hours without a break on winter Saturdays *and* I have to take work home.

This morning I was lying in bed and thinking about the big winners that we had to pay, and that we wouldn't have enough money, and whether it was better to go to the bank or another shop to get some, and whether I should get it before we opened, or after.

I was just going to get up when I realised that I had settled Tom's accumulator wrongly. He had six 50p doubles, four 50p trebles and £1 accumulator but I had settled it all for 50p units.

Not only do we take work home, we take it to bed with us!

Tuesday 23rd November

We got two letters from head office this morning.

Both were dated last week, both were sent first-class and both were posted yesterday, the day postal charges went up.

The importance of one is reflected by my having forgotten what it was all about, whilst the other one concerned unnecessary expenditure and the need to economise!

Wednesday 24th November

I was on holiday for the last managers' meeting but my luck ran out today.

Neil arrived with great rolls of new posters which he distributed among us.

They were all about the various bets we take, but he explained that there were two different ones that he hadn't managed to get hold of.

Unfortunately, the ones about efficient office procedures had been mislaid! That raised a laugh.

As for the health and safety posters, Alice, the D.M.'s secretary had these and had intended to drive over and give them to Neil, but she had an accident at work yesterday and was off sick.

"What ever did she do?" asked Maureen.

"I'm not sure," said Neil.

"I bet I know," said Dave, "she tripped over the health and safety posters!"

Thursday 25th November

We received details of the Christmas Dinner/Dance.

This is usually the one social event that is talked about for the next twelve months, not because of the excellent food or the boring speeches, but for which section manager got drunk and made a fool of himself.

Friday 26th November

We had a special offer today, adding five points to the S.P. of all the outsiders.

I asked Margaret to explain this as she paid out on such bets as I didn't want the customers thinking that they had been overpaid and having a guilty conscience!

"That's very generous," said one lucky punter, "I expect you'll be registering as a charity soon!"

Saturday 27th November

My fears that I should be left short-staffed on Saturdays since Jill left have so far proved groundless. The P.M. has sent me Sheila who gets on very well with Margaret.

They are both of a similar age and both have grown-up children, and grandchildren.

Although we are busy, there are always some odd moments for them to talk in between serving customers and their topic of conversation this afternoon was 'men'.

Not the lovey-dovey chat of young women but the mature talk of grandmothers whose experience extends beyond fathers and husbands to sons and sons-in-law.

This conversation consisted of a catalogue of their experiences with 'the weaker sex', which are briefly summed up thus:

> "Men never do a job when you ask them; they always have to finish reading the paper, or have a smoke first."

> "Men will do anything for you when you are ill but if you make the mistake of saying that you feel a little better, they expect you to carry on where you left off."
>
> "Generally speaking, men are pretty useless although some are more useless than others."

I have to admit that I could see myself in some of their criticisms.

When my mother-in-law cried when I married her daughter, I thought it was because she was so happy for her, but perhaps I was mistaken!

Monday 29th November

A memo arrived informing us that the system for paying out on tickets from other branches will soon be changed.

At present, we have a list of local shops but for those in other areas we have to ring a shop in our district to get the phone number of the one we want.

Managers have always said that it was crazy to make a phone call to *one* shop to get the phone number of *another* shop and it would be a *good* idea if we all had a list.

Upper-management always responded to this by saying that it would be too expensive, but having had several years to think about it, they have concluded that it is crazy to make a phone call to *one* shop to get the phone number of *another* shop, so we will all be getting a complete list in the New Year.

I suppose they view this as another of their *brilliant* ideas!

Tuesday 30th November

Steve was in today. He's training a new puppy.

"Sit," he said, and the dog did what he was told for five seconds, then got up and went for a wander round the shop.

When Steve noticed, he went after it and made him sit again.

This happened several times but each time the dog didn't remain sitting for long.

Just as Steve was going to impose his will again, Margaret called over to him. "Have a heart. How would you like to sit on a cold floor with no trousers on!?"

DECEMBER 1993

Another joke wasted – Revenge is sweet – The perfect gift – Expensive economising – How one manager could be as sick as a parrot! – An easy number? – The D.M. cheers us all up – Margaret is not easily shocked! – A troublesome door – Odd odds – A black day! – Not the best Christmas promotion – A working holiday – I get the blues! – I hear of a couple of disasters – An impossible dream? – A helpful delivery – Business inefficiency – Jeff's final insult. I'm hurt.

Wednesday 1st December

Margaret asked the P.M. last week, for Wednesday, Thursday and Friday off, this week, as she wanted to do some Christmas shopping.

"No problem," he said, "I'll soon sort something out."

So he asked Sheila to come instead, forgetting that he had already promised her Thursday off.

He rang me this morning with his usual tale of woe – this was his worst week and he didn't know what to do and would I say to Sheila when she came in that if she could possibly manage to work tomorrow after all, she could have Saturday off instead.

I put this to her when she arrived but the answer was still "No," so I rang the P.M. and told him that despite my threatening Sheila with thumbscrews she said that she couldn't work.

However, the P.M. was in no mood to appreciate my humour.

Thursday 2nd December

I paid a customer £134.50 for £1 yankee with three winners and a loser.

"It's a pleasure to pay you out," I told him.

"You wouldn't have said that if the other one had won," he replied.

"Well, actually," I said, "I like paying out the firm's money. I feel that I'm getting my own back!"

Friday 3rd December

I was pleased to see Sheila back again.

"Who did you have yesterday?" she asked.

"Oh, they sent four people to replace you," I said.

(Actually, they got someone from another district to come by taxi. It cost £20 each way and I expect that I will get the blame for being overspent on my expenses budget.)

Saturday 4th December

Pat asked me what I wanted for Christmas and I said "snow".

She said that was very anti-social of me wanting to inflict that on everyone, so I said that I would settle for six inches at Ayr, Hereford, Huntingdon, Kempton, Market Rasen, Newton Abbot, Sedgefield, Wetherby, Wincanton and Wolverhampton, which by coincidence are all due to stage meetings on Boxing Day.

Pat said that she couldn't promise anything but she would see what she could do.

Monday 6th December

It's leaked out that the D.M. is getting paid bonuses for cutting out unnecessary expenses.

We could save his wages for a start.

Tuesday 7th December

I heard that some part-time cashiers left last week after being made redundant. Apparently the D.M. has decided that we're overstaffed!

Wednesday 8th December

Both cashiers at one of our prestige shops phoned in yesterday to say that they were ill and would not be in.

Because of staff redundancies, the Personnel Manager spent an anxious morning ringing round other districts to get replacements.

It cost £5 in phone calls and £35 in taxi fares to staff the shop.

Thursday 9th December

The D.M. has banned staff from getting taxis at the firm's expense.

Friday 10th December

Margaret went sick so I rang the P.M. to see about a relief cashier.

The only person available was Tina who was looking after a shop while the manager was at the dentist's.

Eventually she got a train and although there was a long row of taxis outside the station she had to walk two miles – in high heels – to my shop, arriving an hour after racing had started, by which time several of my best customers had left and gone to our rivals in town because of the limited service in my shop.

Later I rang the P.M. to tell him that by some miracle I *hadn't* got a migraine but this was hardly the best treatment for someone with a stress problem.

He wasn't there. *He* had gone home with a migraine!

Saturday 11th December

The night of the Christmas Dinner/Dance.

On Thursday the D.M. had undergone a minor eye operation and then yesterday he had fallen over and twisted his knee.

But nothing was going to keep him away from the festivities so he arrived on crutches and wearing an eye patch.

Needless to say this prompted a lot of conversation about parrots which produced a lot of loud guffaws as though someone had cracked an extremely original joke instead of one that's probably been knocking around for over a hundred years.

However, I admired the manager who went up to the D.M. and apologised, saying that he didn't realise that we were meant to go in fancy dress!

As we're already short-staffed I don't think the perpetrator of this brazen remark will be made to walk the plank, although he might find himself marooned, not on a desert island, but in the grottiest shop in the district!

Monday 13th December

A lot of people think that managing a betting-shop is a doddle –

we start at ten (never mind getting the shop ready), then sit at a desk settling a few bets and reading the paper; then after a lengthy lunch-break, we sit at our desk again and settle a few more bets until it's time to go home at 5.30 p.m.

In reality we work long hours, often without a break, and often without overtime pay, and those of us who manage small shops with only one cashier get plenty of exercise in our sitting down jobs!

Tuesday 14th December

The D.M.'s a genius.

Who says so?

He does, of course.

Not in so many words, but at today's managers' meeting, where he made a guest appearance, he issued us with a list of all the things that have to be done each day before 11.30.

When I complained that I was often on my own in the mornings and would not always have time, he said that he had allowed for that.

He told us that when he last managed a shop, it took him five minutes to put up the papers and fifteen minutes to do a board display.

As it takes me at least a quarter of an hour to put up the papers, I should have asked him for some of his co-operative drawing pins; mine are very contrary and jump out of the pinboards and hide in the darkest corners.

As for board displays, I would like to work in a place similar to the D.M.'s old shop where the phone never rang and all the customers stood around waiting for him to finish his art-work before troubling him with their bets.

Wednesday 15th December

The D.M. is going to give us all a long break over Christmas.

He's going on holiday!

Thursday 16th December

It was raining. A customer came in and gave Margaret his bets.

"These slips are wet," she said, "I can't ring them up on the till – I might get electrocuted!"

Friday 17th December

How one door can cause so much trouble is amazing.

It all started eight years ago when our premises were converted into a betting-shop. We had a nice new door but unfortunately someone forgot that we would need a letterbox!

The door pushed open both ways but when pushed to leave, it partly obscured the step outside and some people missed their footing.

So we called in our odd-job man who fitted a 'stop' on the doorframe so it only opened inwards.

Then it banged shut and the vibrations dislodged the tiles on the outside wall so we had to have one of those things fitted to the top of the door to make it close slowly. (My technical knowledge is almost non-existent and I don't know what it's called). But then it was hard to open – and it still banged.

But the one problem that we haven't been able to solve satisfactorily is that if it rains, water tends to get underneath the door.

This is conveniently soaked up by our daily delivery of newspapers!

It rained last night so when I got in I wasn't surprised to see a pile of sodden papers surrounded by a lake.

One way to dry them out is to put them up on the pinboards in the normal way, although this is easier said than done as they tend to disintegrate in your hands.

When they dry out, they tend to look like I feel at the end of a busy day – a bit limp!

Saturday 18th December

I don't know why they have to have such peculiar odds in South Africa – 3/5, 7/10, 9/5.

Why can't they bet like us – 20/21, 10/11, 85/40?

Monday 20th December

It rained again overnight which meant another lot of soggy papers.

When they are wet, the newsprint comes off on your hands and you end up looking as though you've spent all night down a coal-mine.

Tuesday 21st December

The firm like me to do some sort of Christmas promotion so I bought eight dozen hot mince pies from the local bakers.

That was the easy part. The hard part was trying to give them away.

Arthur took half a dozen which he gave to his dog, who must have thought that it was his lucky day as he gobbled them all down in less than two minutes.

Otherwise, there was little interest and I ended up giving 75 cold mince pies to the Methodist Church for their old people's party.

I don't reckon on a lot of free publicity from there.

Wednesday 22nd December

Arthur came in and accused me of making his dog sick!

Thursday 23rd December

The start of our Christmas holiday.

Although I was off, I still called at the shop this morning to settle the bets from the dog meetings not covered by Teletext and to put up the decorations.

Despite writing out notices explaining that we were not open today, despite there being no racing, despite the shop being in darkness, and despite having the 'closed' sign up, a dozen people tried the door in the hour I was there.

When I left I walked along the parade to the off-licence to get some cans, just in case we have visitors next week. We don't usually and I end up having them myself, so I only got drinks that I like.

On leaving the off-licence, I saw Old Joe rattling the door of my shop; then he looked through the letter-box, scratched his head and tried the door again, before giving up and going to the pub.

Then I met Arthur who asked me if the racing was off today. I told him that it wasn't off because it wasn't on, but I think that only confused him.

This afternoon, I drove into town to do some Christmas shopping and met Jim who complained that he had called at the betting-shop only to find it closed.

Then I met Harry who was similarly disappointed. He was with his wife and they both had trolleys laden with enough food and drink to withstand a siege, but to hear him complain about how he couldn't collect his winnings, you would have thought that this was all he had in the world and he wouldn't be able to eat until he collected it on Monday.

We get to know the regulars' bets and I remember settling his. He's got £2.50 to come!

Friday 24th December

I drove into town to call at my bank. They love me there. Most people cash cheques in multiples of a tenner but I always make mine out for silly amounts, killing two birds with one stone by getting change for work which I then swap for larger denominations for the housekeeping money.

I got £73 out today and the bank clerk didn't seem too happy as he gave me £40 of 50ps, £20 of 20ps, £5 of 10ps, £5 of 5ps, £2 of 2ps and £1 of 1ps, but then maybe he was tired. He had been counting out money since 9.30 a.m. and it was then 11.55 a.m.

He should have been pleased as they were due to close at noon. Two and a half hours' work – it was hardly worth going in for.

However, I was glad that he made the effort.

Then I went to the betting-shop with the change.

I was just going to open the door when I saw Jeff.

JOCKS
RUIN
Best

"Hiya Gus," he said, "I'm just going to buy a paper, I feel lucky today."

"It's a pity there's no racing," I said.

"Has it all been cancelled then?" he exclaimed.

So I reminded him that there was never any racing on Christmas Eve and that we were closed.

"What, another day off?" shouted Jeff.

I did a few jobs at the shop. It was quite difficult settling the last of the dog bets with all the lights off, but I didn't want to appear to be open. As it was, fourteen people tried the door.

Saturday 25th December

CHRISTMAS DAY

My family know that two of my favourite colours are blue and gold so Pat bought me a blue shirt, a blue jumper and three pairs of blue socks.

The kids got me a bottle of gold-coloured liquid with a Christmassy ring to it and a blue bobble-hat, which is not exactly what the best-dressed betting-shop manager is wearing this season, but it will sure keep the bald bonce warm.

Sunday 26th December

I asked Colin, Dave and their wives to our house for a drink this evening.

I told them about my disastrous Christmas promotion and Colin said that he had a similar experience.

He had organised a free raffle with a Christmas cake as the prize.

Unfortunately the winner put his cake on a chair, someone sat on it and a fight broke out.

This was a nice piece of timing as it coincided with what was to have been a friendly visit by the police.

It was a pity that the law hadn't visited my shop instead. They could have had a mince pie!

Monday 27th December

Joe Loudmouth was in this morning. He said that he called at the shop last Thursday to back three dogs at the night meetings but we were closed.

Then he drove all round the district, spending a fiver on petrol and getting a parking ticket, in an effort to find a betting-shop that was open.

He failed – and, of course, they all won.

Tuesday 28th December

I was settling one of our exclusive multiple bets this afternoon and wondering whether to blame the idiot who sits in his ivory tower all day thinking up such complicated bets, or the idiot who had the bet and then handed in his ticket as soon as the last selection had run.

My calculations were complicated because the bet included two selections that were subject to 'Rule 4' (7/4 became 1.3125 to 1 and 6/4 became 1.35 to 1), and the fact that the '5' on my calculator kept sticking.

This got me thinking that if there are betting-shops in the next world, in the warmer place, all the bets would be like this and all the labour-saving equipment would be faulty.

I hope, therefore, to lead a blameless life and qualify for the other place where it's warm in winter and cool in summer, and where all the odds are evens or something to one and where there's no Rule 4.

And maybe we would get an hour for lunch on Saturdays!

Wednesday 29th December

The manager of the shop next door brought me a parcel. It had been left with him last Thursday because we were closed and it was too big to go through the letter box.

He hadn't been able to deliver it before because he had been shut since Christmas.

On opening it I found two identical posters which announced that we would be closed last Thursday, Friday and Saturday!

Thursday 30th December

The end of the year stock-take revealed that we have got 497 small brown envelopes that we don't normally use and *no* big brown ones that we do use.

We've also got 44 gross of punters' pens and 62 felt-tips.

Attempts to redistribute these to other shops have failed as they have all got too many as well.

Friday 31st December

Jeff, who had been away for Christmas, called in today.

"Oh no," I said to him jokingly, "what are you doing back so soon?"

"The Christmas spirit has soon worn off here," remarked someone.

"Gus never had any," said Jeff, "they modelled Scrooge on him."

I didn't think that was very nice. *I* never make fun of anybody.